HINCH
VS
CANBERRA

BEHIND THE HUMAN HEADLINES

DERRYN HINCH

MELBOURNE
UNIVERSITY
PRESS

Thank you

To all of you who believed enough in the cause of justice to vote for me. This was the first year, as we tried to 'keep the bastards honest'.

MELBOURNE UNIVERSITY PRESS
An imprint of Melbourne University Publishing Limited
Level 1, 715 Swanston Street, Carlton, Victoria 3053, Australia
mup-contact@unimelb.edu.au
www.mup.com.au

First published 2017
Text © Derryn Hinch, 2017
Design and typography © Melbourne University Publishing Limited, 2017

All previously published columns originally appeared in *Crikey*. All unattributed photos are the author's own.

Cover design by Philip Campbell Design
Typeset by Megan Ellis
Printed in Australia by McPherson's Printing Group

A catalogue record for this book is available from the National Library of Australia

9780522873177 (paperback)
9780522873184 (ebook)

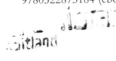

CONTENTS

THE GOOD, THE BAD AND THE UGLY

I've met every prime minister since Bob Menzies—all fourteen of them. And I've interviewed hundreds of politicians and would-be politicians over the decades.

So, I guess I am sort of equipped to rate my Canberra confrères, and protagonists, after my first year on the Hill (with more detail to come in my diaries).

Here they are, in no order of import, impact or relevance, in about 100 words or less.

MALCOLM TURNBULL

It was lyrical to tag the PM 'Malcolm in a muddle', as I did, when the Tony Abbott sniping escalated, the conservatives hog-tied him and his much-vaunted policies stalled. I invoked legendary Hawthorn coach John Kennedy: 'Do something!' Do a Gough, I urged him: 'Crash through or crash.' Be the man remembered for bringing Australia marriage equality or solving the energy crisis. Something. In person, he was genuine, and honest in his dealings with me. Without his help, I would not have got the passport ban on convicted paedophiles signed into law within seven months.

BILL SHORTEN

With Turnbull's torpor in the polls putting his leadership on thin ice, Bill Shorten started being called the Steven Bradbury of Canberra. I did write it was a mite early for him and Chloe, his wife, to be measuring curtains for the Lodge, because he still lagged in the polls as preferred PM. And then there's the cutting smear, first aimed at failed British Labour leader Ed Miliband, that has been applied to Shorten: 'How can you believe a word he says, when his own face doesn't believe him?' Still, Shorten was great in his support of me as chair of the joint National Redress Committee, to operate as watchdog over the government's reaction to the *Royal Commission into Institutional Responses to Child Sexual Abuse.*

TONY ABBOTT

Long before Tony Abbott became prime minister, I was one of those commentators who dubbed him the 'Mad Monk'. Since being rolled as PM, Abbott has been a bigger, more acerbic, critic of his successor than even Bill Shorten. I suspect Malcolm Turnbull has continued the clerical theme by thinking 'Who will rid me of this meddlesome priest?' I was on the receiving end of an Abbott phone-message blast after reporting his supporters were leaking to Shorten. He told me to produce evidence or 'shut the fuck up'. As well, Abbott's leadership of the same-sex marriage 'No' campaign has, at times, been unhinged.

SCOTT MORRISON

It would be glib, and easy, to say everything is 'slow-mo with ScoMo' when the economy has been sluggish and wages stubbornly low. But stop the quotes. Apart from a personal hiccup with the backpacker tax, I found the treasurer good to deal with. No flim-flam, no bullshit. As the year wore on, the pragmatism of the Turnbull team was reflected in it actually getting some stuff through the Senate. A long way, I'm told, from the chest-poking 'My way or the highway' Abbott approach to senators. Couldn't abide Morrison's Hillsong-style opposition to same-sex marriage, though.

MATHIAS CORMANN

I know some people are tempted to spell Cormann with a K—as in 'kraut'—which is unfair because the senator is/was

Belgian. I'll concede, Cormann does have a Germanic manner in the chamber, but I have found him to be one of the best, most straightforward, people to deal with on the government frontbench. He is pragmatic and, if some parts of an omnibus bill are obviously on the nose, he will summarily say, 'Park it … park it.' Meaning that amendment will not see the light of day again this parliamentary term.

MALCOLM ROBERTS

The truncated, in more ways than one, (now former) One Nation senator I found to be a pleasant-enough fellow—except for his fruit-bat behaviour over the dual-citizenship issue. As the crossbench planned to refer his case to the High Court, and before he fell on his own sword, I went to see Roberts to get his story. After what I would hear later, I declined to call him a 'liar' in the chamber but did say he'd been 'extremely economical with the truth'. Roberts did bring the term 'empirical evidence' into the Senate lexicon. In the supplicant prayers we have in the Senate every morning, I wanted to shout to him, 'Where's the empirical evidence?'

PAULINE HANSON

She is a genuine enigma. Loved by many, loathed by some. And she's been around in politics for twenty years, for Christ's sake. In the old days, a novice, manipulated by cynical operatives, Pauline Hanson, back with a bloc of four One Nation senators, now has real voting power. She doesn't like me. We were sparring partners on *Sunrise* on Channel Seven until she started making excuses, and then refused to appear with me at all. Hanson has a blotting-paper ability to absorb figures; get her off-guard and she is a startled rabbit caught in the headlights. Not that bright.

PENNY WONG

One of my Senate favourites—the leader of the opposition in that bear pit (as Neville Wran used to call parliament); George Brandis's conscience. She will take, and trust, you at your word, which isn't common in that often venal place. She commands respect on both sides of the fighting field.

I have only one reservation. Years ago, I saw Penny Wong on *Q&A* defending then prime minister Julia Gillard's 'marriage is only for a man and a woman' argument. I ached for Wong to resign and go to the backbench on principle— like Andrew Peacock did over Pol Pot and Kampuchea. But I trust her, more than most.

JULIE BISHOP

It's a tired old political joke (and even more so for females) but it applies to Julie Bishop: always the bridesmaid and never the bride. Forget bouquet-catching. You can't be deputy to four party leaders (two of them being Malcolm Turnbull) and dream you'll ever get the top job. And Bishop won't— although she got a taste as acting prime minister when the High Court benched Barnyard Barnaby and the PM went to Beersheba. She is a clever, shrewd person/politician and, I suspect, a good foreign minister. She knows bullshit when it is lobbed our way. And she has been very supportive of me on curbing the activities of paedophile 'child rape' tourists.

MICHAELIA CASH

Ah, Michaelia. Nobody in parliament walks faster than her, except the Greens' peripatetic Rachel Siewert. And Cash can duck and swerve as adroitly in negotiations on industrial relations as she does in the corridors. The eyelashes may flutter but there is steel in there, as you can see when she takes on the Construction, Forestry, Mining and Energy Union, and Shorten's connections to it, on the Senate floor. Cash needed all her ducking and swerving talents at Senate estimates after denying her staff had alerted media to AFP raids on the AWU. We have had some tough head-to-heads before finally agreeing on amendments but they've always makes me think of that line from the Marilyn Monroe movie *Some Like it Hot*: 'Daphne, you're leading again!'

NICK XENOPHON

When it comes to Senator Xenophon, I've amended an old adage, to 'Beware of Greeks, not bearing, but accepting, gifts.' You always have to be aware that the leader of the Xenophon team is a clever dealmaker, and one with a government that needs him. We get on well. When I joined Xenophon, and the impressive Skye Kakoschke-Moore and Stirling Griff, to provide a powerful bloc of four votes on one issue, an Adelaide newspaper called us 'The Four Amigos'. And, at times, we will be. Especially on social issues that are often, callously, disregarded by the major parties. It didn't surprise me that Xenapom survived the High Court but it did when he quit to go back to state politics.

STEPHEN PARRY

He was the good, then things went bad and it got ugly. The Senate president was one of the most impressive people I met on the Hill. He was fair, learned and well-ordered in the chamber. A respected and tranquil chairman in meetings. He would have been the last senator (apart from me) I'd have thought would be caught up in the dual citizenship scandal. In the wake of Fiona Nash's antecedents (which mirrored his own) his tardiness in coming forward tainted his reputation.

CORY BERNARDI

I have one fundamental problem when it comes to Senator Bernardi. I believe it is unethical to stand as a top-of-ticket Senate candidate for one party and, within months, flee the coop, quit the Liberals and announce your new conservative party—especially when you've just spent months, in a taxpayer-funded sinecure, as an observer at the United Nations. I get on well with Bernardi but there's a 'main chancer' element there that disturbs me. He does support the dugongs and sea turtles, though. The man has a heart.

GEORGE BRANDIS

Let me get an anti-Brandis story out of the way. One day, we were walking out of a crossbench meeting, which George had chaired. One of his stovepipe-trousered male aides was behind us. Imperiously, Brandis thrust a folder behind him, like it was a baton. The aide captured it. The federal attorney-general strode on. I thought, 'What an arrogant prick.' Having said that, I think Brandis's question time performance is a daily gem. Brilliant. In conversation, he is charming. He won't have to buy new suits if, as rumoured, he goes to London.

ERIC ABETZ

Sometimes they stay too long after the lights go down. I had a moment with Senator Abetz that, I'll confess, colours my attitude towards this ultra-conservative relic. One day, he sidled up to me on the red leather and kindly asked the rookie about his living arrangements. I was thinking about renting or buying an apartment in Canberra but eventually opted to stay in a hotel.

Abetz earnestly told me about how, for his first twelve years in Canberra, he had boarded with a 'little old lady' who washed and ironed his shirts and cooked him dinner. And Eric voted against marriage equality?

SAM DASTYARI

When, or if, you deign to analyse Senator Dastyari, I suggest you first dig out a novel called *What Makes Sammy Run?* about a 'hard mover', as Melbourne people would call him. We all know Dastyari is a hard mover, a shaker, a party broker. But his confessions of culpability and mea culpa stance get him off the hook. No other pollie could have survived his excruciating 'I'm so sorry' press conference after the scandal over him accepting Chinese money. He has a genuine heart, though. And I ducked his kiss on the mouth.

DAVID LEYONHJELM

Mr Leyonhjelm makes life easy for you in the Senate if you just accept that he is the most intelligent person there. Which, actually, is not that easy to do. He *is* clever. A very shrewd man. In the first place, the logo for his Liberal Democratic Party, and its position on the ballot paper, fooled lots of Libs into voting for his party by mistake. As a libertarian, I've warmed to him but he can be capricious. And it will always be David first.

JACQUI LAMBIE

I know that she won't disagree when I say that Senator Lambie has the foulest mouth, the dirtiest vocab, of anybody I have ever met. She'd blister the walls off a wharfies' hut. But I related to her more than most senators before her shock dual citizenship resignation. I chastised her for being so close to Labor that she was regarded as its twenty-seventh Senate vote. But Jacqui has a huge heart. She stumbled, passionately, in the Senate but her love and work for our war vets must be commended. Jacqui Lambie was the best weapon our defence force has ever seen.

IAN MACDONALD

There's a revered position called 'Father of the Senate'. It is currently held by Senator Ian Macdonald. He's also, I'm told, Father of the Parliament, since Philip Ruddock has gone. (I'm the oldest-ever elected senator but that doesn't count.) Senator Macdonald chairs several important Senate committees. At one, where he was niggled by Greens senator Nick McKim, Macdonald turned on Senate opposition leader Penny Wong. In a private corridor, Macdonald told Wong to 'grow up' and to stop throwing tantrums. As a newcomer, I was stunned by this disrespect and wrote to the Senate president about it. His biggest attempts to insult me were 'you're such a limited person' and 'outside of Melbourne nobody knows who you are'.

CHRISTOPHER PYNE

Last, and probably least, we have Mr Paaaarn. The Liberal brains trust member who actually, on air, called the Libs an 'election-winning machine' as they came within one seat of losing government in 2016.

It is that sort of seriously detached posturing that makes me cringe. Makes me ponder a Labor victory at the next federal election.

To be fair, Pyne and I have nothing to do with each other, as we're in opposite houses of parliament. But I hope the PM reins him in.

HOW THE HELL DID THAT HAPPEN?

It was a cold, grey and drizzly morning in March 2014. I was standing in front of a media scrum outside Langi Kal Kal prison in country Victoria, after serving fifty days of imprisonment for contempt of court in the case against Adrian Bayley for the rape and murder of Jill Meagher.

The jail time (including two weeks in solitary confinement in a small cell at the Melbourne Assessment Prison) was triggered by my refusal to pay a $100000 fine—the largest contempt fine ever for an individual in Victoria. Probably in Australia.

It was less than three years since I'd served five months under house arrest, wearing an electronic monitor ankle bracelet, for breaching a suppression order and naming two notorious serial child abusers on the steps of Victoria's Parliament House. About 5000 other people shouted their names too but I was the only one charged. That house-arrest sentence also cost me my job at 3AW.

There was a question from the pack outside Langi Kal Kal: 'So, what do you do next?'

What indeed? More than a year earlier, I had launched a petition for a national public register of convicted sex offenders and got 70000 signatures. But no state government had expressed much interest except for the Northern Territory's.

One afternoon, I stood in my Melbourne apartment, tears in my eyes. The NT attorney-general and minister for justice, John Elferink, was on speaker phone. With him, in his Darwin office, were Bruce and Denise Morcombe, parents of murdered Queensland schoolboy Daniel.

Elferink wanted us to share the news that legislation for the first public register in Australia—resembling Megan's Law, which President Bill Clinton had made federal US law in 1996 and involved having a public national register of convicted sex offenders, including details of their crimes, sentences, photos and home addresses—had been introduced to the NT parliament and was about to be enacted. Within weeks, civil rights activists, political weaklings and legal eagles had scuttled it.

After being sacked by 3AW at the end of 2012 (because they were 'sick of this paedophile thing—and so are the listeners') I rejoined the Seven Network to do stories for *Sunday Night* and *Today Tonight*. One of my assignments was to go to the United States to do a series of interviews about the sex offenders register and how it worked.

In Hamilton, New Jersey, a picturesque little town like something from a Norman Rockwell painting, I interviewed Maureen Kanka. She was the mother of Megan, a 7-year-old girl who was raped and murdered by paroled rapist Jesse Timmendequas, who lived across the street and whose criminal history was unknown to the law-abiding folk of the township.

In her grief and anger, Megan's mother made it her mission to get a public register up and running in New Jersey. In 1996, President Clinton invited Maureen, and her husband, Richard, to the Oval Office to watch it become national law.

In Florida, I interviewed a sheriff who had had local prisoners make big red and white metal signs, which were cemented into the front lawns of former prisoners, warning people that a convicted sex offender lived there. Also in Florida, I visited a caravan park that was home to more than 100 convicted paedophiles. I interviewed ten of them, at a site clearly marked as the home of sex criminals, with signs warning that unaccompanied children were not permitted there.

In the midst of this, a New Zealand *60 Minutes* reporter asked me about rehabilitation of child sex offenders. She zealously inquired, 'You don't believe in rehabilitation, do you?'

While it may seem unfair to have used it as a debating point, I knew my interviewer had a young daughter. I said,

'Would you let a rehabilitated paedophile babysit your child?' Her stunned non-answer was my answer.

In San Antonio, Texas, I interviewed former child actor Sarah Monahan, who played Jenny Kelly in the Seven Network sitcom *Hey Dad..!*. During this time, she was abused by her screen father, played by actor Robert Hughes, who is now behind bars in Goulburn.

In 1988–92, the *Hinch* program was often broadcast from an adjacent studio at Epping in Sydney. Sarah told me, decades later, how, as an abused child, she had wanted to come and talk to me but was never allowed near our studio. In Texas, she showed me an iPhone app into which she typed the words 'sex offender'. And up came eight or so flags; a bit like if she'd typed the word 'motel'. The app showed the names, photographs, home addresses and crimes of all convicted sex offenders living in that area.

We drove past the address of one of the men listed on the app. It was a neat and normal suburban house. A well-trimmed lawn, a pick-up truck in the driveway, and an American flag fluttering by the front porch. No vigilantes, no Molotov cocktail throwers.

'It just means that you can warn your child not to chase a ball into that yard and not to go there for trick or treat at Hallowe'en,' Sarah explained. Or, as in Megan Kanka's case, to be wary when a neighbour invites you in to 'look at a cute puppy'. I tried the app out again in Times Square in Manhattan and about ten flags came up within a few blocks of 42nd Street.

Ironically, it was a Channel Seven connection that put me on a path that would, ultimately, send me to Canberra. When news of my 3AW sacking made page one of the *Herald Sun*, Lewis Martin, Seven's managing director in Melbourne, immediately called and offered me a job, but also asked the question I'd been asked outside Langi Kal Kal. 'So, what do you do next?'

He wasn't talking about radio or television but about the campaign for a public register of convicted sex offenders, and other justice issues. Martin suggested a symbolic walk. I came up with the 'Jail 2 Justice' title and my partner, Natasha Chadwick, plotted the detailed ten-day route from outside Langi Kal Kal to the steps of Parliament House in Melbourne, where we would present volumes of petition signatures, with more we had collected along the way.

Before beginning the walk, we meticulously drove the route, planned which motels and hotels we would stay in, and the back-road routes that would safely keep the marchers off major highways. It was on that reconnoitre that Natasha took the 'Johnny Cash' photo on this book's cover of my walking along an abandoned railway line alongside a decrepit old station outside Beaufort, Victoria.

It was a fantastic, if at times disturbing, daily ritual, with sometimes fifty, sometimes several hundred, supporters, and on the last day, when we walked from where Jill Meagher was murdered in Brunswick to Parliament House in Spring Street, several thousand. Including about a dozen women pushing their vulnerable little kids in prams.

I say 'disturbing', because the campaigners all had personal stories to tell. Heading into Ballarat, the local police chief joined me. I said: 'There are 200 people behind us and they all have stories to share. None of them good ones.' He agreed. He also told me there were more than 120 released prisoners on the private sex offenders register in his region.

He echoed what a senior VicPol officer had told me: 'The register's a joke. A public relations exercise to make people feel good.' The officer pointed out that if he visited three offenders a day, and did no other police work, he couldn't check up on them all even once a month. Mostly, they 'self-reported' a change of job or address.

The 'What next?' question cropped up a lot on that long walk and I had plenty of time to think. Getting into politics had never been on the Hinch 'must do' list. I'd built a reputation questioning and attacking politicians. Now, listeners and viewers were suggesting I become one.

That element of 'If you can't lick 'em, join 'em' was appealing, and I was starting to accept I wasn't going to get anywhere with that public register just by broadcasting about it and lobbying for it from the outside. John Elferink's phone call had raised and crushed hopes for me and the Morcombes—who had joined me on the final leg of the Jail 2 Justice walk to Parliament House.

It wasn't quite like in the idealistic American movie *Mr. Smith Goes to Washington* but there were traces of that. On 26 May 2014, after ten days and 180 kilometres, walking about 20 kilometres a day, we presented eleven volumes, with more than 125 000 signatures, to a state government rep on the steps of Parliament House.

Then, on a Sunday night in September 2015, Natasha Chadwick and my friend and PA, Annette Philpott (whom I'd earlier taken into my confidence), and I, sat in my living room for a tactical all-nighter. We pushed the buttons that sent live a website with a video announcement of a new dynamic in Australian politics—Derryn Hinch's Justice Party.

I had planned a traditional media event. Send out a press release. Invite the TV cameras and scribes along. To paraphrase the movie *Field of Dreams*: 'Build it and they will come.' Natasha, who had cleverly built the JP website, and shot my 'I'm Derryn Hinch and I'm going into politics' video, convinced me to concentrate totally on social media. It was pervasive, it was strong and it was cheap. And we didn't have much money.

By 7 a.m. Channel Nine was running the video on their news bulletins. By 10 a.m., as we were hastily sticking up posters in our tiny Queens Road, Melbourne, office, the TV crews were knocking on the door.

We were off and running but there were a couple of snags: we had to get 500 official members and I had to get elected to the Senate. Before the 2016 election, Malcolm Turnbull and the Greens had done a shonky deal over preferences to make things that much harder for small parties and independents.

In May 2016, Prime Minister Turnbull called the election for 2 July, with a ludicrous, and dangerous (for the government), marathon campaign. That time allowed us to clock up 11 250 kilometres aboard the campaign van we dubbed the Justice Bus, travelling through country Victoria and parts of New South Wales.

By March 2016, we had a registered party. On 2 July 2016, Victoria had a new senator.

Hinch vs Canberra was on.

And this is my diary record of that first year.

SENATE DIARY

FIRST DAY OF SCHOOL

25 August 2016

Apologies to writer Guy Rundle (and maybe Hunter S Thompson) but, in the middle of my first day of Senate School in Canberra, my mind obscurely flashed to Winston Churchill. Maybe it was because I'd been staying in the Curtin Room, and later the Menzies Suite, at the Hyatt Canberra. But, anyhow, the British bulldog came to mind in the massive committee room I was herded into with all the other freshmen (and freshwomen) senators.

I was one of only 591 men and (shamefully few) women who have ever held the honorific 'Senator' in this Commonwealth of Australia. A far more exclusive club than for those who have worn the Baggy Green or played for the VFL/AFL.

Sitting there (wearing my exclusive 'access all areas' senator's lapel button, which negates the need for a security pass) and clutching my *Pocket Guide to Senate Procedure*, I thought of Winnie, who once said, 'I am always ready to learn, although I do not always like being taught.'

Know how you feel, Winston.

It was my first time back at school since 1959. That's fifty-seven years ago. More than 20 000 days ago. I didn't know what a 'high school drop-out' was until I went to America and discovered that I was one.

But here I was, for two-and-a-half days a week, back in school. The most famous/notorious/infamous other student at this political seminary was Pauline Hanson. We were two frosty seats apart.

She came with her quartet of accidentally elected Pauline Hanson's One Nation (PHON) stalwarts. Sounds irreverent, but Pauline, as the leader of the pack, reminded me (in Canberra) of the movie *Grease*. Certainly not Sandy. Betty Rizzo. Expelled from her last school. Bad reputation.

After day one of Senate School, the One Nation quartet went off (actually, Malcolm 'empirical evidence' Roberts asked for an early mark) to meet with the prime minister. Wallpaper: That would have been a meeting of the minds!

I'm told somebody asked Hanson if she had 'worked Senator Hinch out yet?' Her response was something like 'I never will.' That's possibly a compliment.

This Canberra immersion has brought back great memories from years and decades past. The last time I was in Canberra, I was in another grand building: the High Court.

The last time I was in the new Parliament House, I sat in the marbled Great Hall for a *Hinch* live interview with prime minister Paul Keating. He joked about growth, and I remember he chided me, and my scepticism, and boasted that if GDP growth couldn't be sustained at 4 per cent, he 'might as well give the game away. I wouldn't deserve to be PM'. They'd kill for 4 per cent now.

What a wonderful town of dreams and spin and bullshit this is. Hinchey, don't let it get to you.

To finish on a serious note, some genuinely tangible stuff. I am making great headway in my quest to pull the passports of convicted sex offenders to stem the child sex tourists in Thailand, Malaysia, Indonesia and the Philippines. Thank you, Rachel Griffiths.

And, within a year, I am confident I will have helped add 1 million more names to the organs donors' register.

The fire is still in the belly. This is exciting. It is an honour. It is awesome.

BEWARE SLEEPERGATE

1 September 2016

If this radical 'Inside (really inside) the Senate' weekly epistle is going to be the real deal, then I must face the most shock! horror! incident in one of the truly biggest moments in my life this week.

I tweeted from inside the Senate (note to self: find out if that's legal): *It's official. Now sworn in as Senator for Victoria in 45th parliament. Now it begins.*

It was an emotional moment. Walking alone down that glass-lined corridor on my way in, I felt the awe and responsibility of it all. As I went to sign the ancient senators' book—the book, not the senators (apart from me)—I did get moist eyes when I looked up at the visitors' gallery at my loyal crew (who started as volunteers for our fledgling Justice Party) and gave them a thumbs up.

It was a huge day. It started with Welcome to Country in the Great Hall, where Bill Shorten (who still thinks he won) spoke longer than the prime minister. Is that protocol cool?

I actually wore a suit and tie. The president of the Senate, Stephen Parry, had briefed us about appropriate attire and said it wasn't compulsory, so I wore a tie of my own free will. Perverse, huh?

At that dos and don'ts briefing from the prez, all the newbies sat in the imposing Senate chamber for the first time. I happened to sit in Arthur Sinodinos's seat. I must admit I opened his drawer. There was no cash in it.

At that dummy run, I realised that I couldn't clearly see the prez. And then, somehow, I chipped a tooth.

So, back in Melbourne on the Saturday, I saw my loyal cosmetic dentist, Yvonne King, for an emergency veneer.

Then my 'senatorial sartorialist', Kelly Casey, who cuts my hair and touches up my beard. And then my optometrist, Helen Robbins, for some trifocals so I can see if Stephen Parry is frowning.

On Opening Day, I had green tea with the PM and got a hug from the foreign affairs minister, Julie Bishop, and a pic with the governor-general, Sir Peter Cosgrove. Malcolm Turnbull has a stunning John Olsen on his wall. From his own collection—not from the Parliament House Aladdin's cave, which senators get to borrow from.

I explained that my friend and former wife, actress Jacki Weaver, and I owned an Olsen from the Lake Eyre collection but the bank thought they needed it more than we did. Like my Mount Macedon farm and vineyard. And a couple of properties in Hawaii.

That will make the pecuniary interests register pretty straightforward.

Cory Bernardi, now leader of the Australian Conservatives, tracked me down in the Senate dining room, where I was lunching with my staff, to get my signature on a bill to remove 'offend' and 'insult' from section 18C. That's my fall-back position, but at least it will get it debated. Issue one.

(Fact check: the bottled water in the Senate dining room is halal-certified. Wonder if Hanson knows? Will she dine there now? Question: how many waterfall throats do they cut and bleed out to get halal water?)

Issue two: I attacked Senate censorship and pounded out an iPad media release announcing my decision to support the press gallery and get the Senate to greenlight more media freedom and oppose archaic restrictions—which don't apply in the lower house—on still photographers taking shots in the Senate.

I said:

People have a right to see exactly what is happening on both sides of the parliament. The media—and thus the public—should be able to see us in action, or photograph our inaction. If you get caught nibbling your ear wax, or counting your money or dozing: tough. We are here to represent the public, and we are paid a lot of money to do it. It is absurd that the media can't effectively show the public exactly what we are up to.

This is not about publicity for me. It's not about more exposure for my bearded mug—this is about the public being entitled to see the people who represent them representing them, even when we're stuffing it up.

And then came the gotcha moment. Sleepergate. Hinch caught with eyes closed during the GG's speech.

I could claim sleep apnoea, from which I suffer. I've overnighted at the Epworth sleep clinic. Tried a CPAP machine. But bugger it … no excuses. I dozed off.

Other people did too as we listened to a rehash of a long, boring speech spoken by a bloke in an ill-fitting suit that looked like a Nikita Khrushchev cast-off. Using other people's words while he talked about 'my government'. We'd heard it all in the marathon election campaign.

Bob Katter later told me that Wayne Swan had elbowed him three times and, on the other side, George Brandis and Christopher Pyne looked suspiciously somnolent.

Using the old Hinch program motto—if you are being run out of town, pretend it's a parade and you're leading it—I can see a silver lining. It also focused attention on the fact that on any other day (because of an Opening Day exemption) the media could not have published that photo. And that is ludicrous censorship.

After the pic went so public, I still introduced a motion to end that censorship.

Not bad after the old man of the seat had been the target of a nanna-nap pap.

HEMINGWAY ON THE HILL

8 September 2016

From now on, for me, the first session of the 45th parliament will be remembered as Hemingway on the Hill: for whom the bell tolls.

The division bells rang, the green lights flashed incessantly on the plethora of corridor clocks, and ten lazy Libs (including several ministers) were exposed playing hooky—more focused on getting an early start to a 10-day break from Canberra than protecting their vulnerable leader from a humiliating string of defeats on the floor of the house.

That amazing photo of Malcolm in a muddle, walking alone through the sea of green leather in an empty chamber, will surely win a Walkley. The classic pic could not have been taken in the Senate, but I'll win that one despite a backseat lecture from Stephen Conroy. It succinctly illustrates my campaign to allow the media the same photographic rights in the Senate as they have in the lower house.

That embarrassing shot of yours truly grabbing some first-day shuteye during the GG's bum-numbing speech at the opening of parliament—which even made it into the

Washington Post—could not have been taken on day two of the parliamentary session.

There was a dispensation for day one.

A pic of Conroy and *moi*, which appeared in the 'Strewth' column in the *Oz* several days later, cleverly makes my point. (To add to the irony, at that frozen pictorial moment, we were discussing my plan to relax the Senate photo-ban rules and bring them into line with the lower house.) *The Australian* could not have legally run that photo—would have incurred the wrath of the Usher of the Black Rod—if they had edited out a bloke in front of us: resources minister Matthew Canavan.

You see, he had 'the call'. And you can legally take pictures of a senator if he, or she, is on their feet. We were mere backdrop material. Noddyland, huh?

Journalist/TV host Paul Barry, on *Media Watch*, supported my campaign to drag this 'august chamber' kicking and screaming into the twenty-first century, although it prompted my tweet: *Media Watch hinting my falling asleep a stunt to help campaign to end Senate photo bans. Wish it were.*

I have support from Senator Mitch Fifield from the Libs and most of the Labor senators. Conroy's resistance, he says, is based on a fear that, in the 'more intimate' Senate chamber, powerful camera lenses could pick up details from confidential documents on senators' desks. I'm told restrictions on such intrusions already apply in the House of Reps. And that's fair.

It seems a compromise is possible, with still cameras permitted to photograph divisions and adjournment debates. Presumably to capture errant Libs dashing off for a long weekend. But that's not good enough.

There's also pressure to push the issue off to a committee. Presumably, similar to that committee (of which leader of the opposition in the Senate Penny Wong was a member) that green-lighted changes that never happened, in 2014.

And still on the Senate. Slippery Sam Dastyari. Or Shanghai Sam, as the Libs have dubbed him.

His transgressions have been well documented, and he gets the Gong of the Month for saying, 'I made a mistake' more times in twenty-five minutes than a Kardashian changes outfits.

He was also just dumb. If he'd asked his Chinese chums for $1000 or $1500 or $2000 as a donation he might have declared it and got away with it. But $1670.82? Duh!

And a word of warning to self as Senator Hinch, even if a non-drinker: never accept a bottle of wine with the name 'Grange' on the label. It never ends well.

I started this epistle with Hemingway, so let's continue the literary bent.

Maybe Sam should read Budd Schulberg's book *What Makes Sammy Run?* about Sammy Glick.

> First, no qualms. Not the thinnest sliver of misgiving about the value of his work. He was as uninhibited as a performing seal. He never questioned his right to monopolize conversations or his ability to do it entertainingly. And then there was his colossal lack of perspective. This was one of his most valuable gifts, for perspective doesn't always pay. It can slow you down.

Or maybe Dastyari should drop in to the Sydney Opera House for the current season of *My Fair Lady*. Remember that line? The one about 'oozing charm' and 'oil'?

★Back to Hemingway and those tolling bells. I can sympathise with fellow politicians who miss divisions. I wear a knee brace after a back-breaking heli-ride mountain accident several years ago. In one bell-ringing episode last week, I made it back into the chamber with forty-four seconds to spare. At least I didn't have to fly back from Melbourne.

WILL HE EVER SIT DOWN?

15 September 2016

Okay, I'll admit it. It was long, far too long. I had trialled my first Senate speech, but obviously, in rehearsal, I had delivered it at the usual Hinch machine-gun rate of around 190 words a minute.

Now, at three-quarters of an hour, it goes into the record books as the longest first speech ever (they are meant to be twenty minutes max) and I'm told I am the first senator called to order by the Senate president when the tradition is for first-timers not to be subjected to interjections.

Nick Xenophon, leader of the Nick Xenophon Team, remonstrated with my staffers about giving me such a clock-busting speech until they pointed out I'd written it myself. It's true: nobody saw it before I delivered it. Not even a lawyer.

Xenophon also offered a journo with fifty-five years of experience any help with editing. But that's Nick.

In the speech, I did make good on my election campaign promise to name names as part of the quest for a national public register of convicted sex offenders.

The biggest boost to that cause came the next day from Victorian police commissioner Graham Ashton, who told Neil Mitchell on 3AW that there was merit in a national public register.

And he admitted, for the first time, that there are more than 6000 names of convicted offenders on the Victorian secret register, which only senior coppers can access. (I thought it was 7000. It's around 9000 in NSW.)

The Commish also admitted that it was impossible for police officers to adequately monitor all the convicted offenders on that list.

In my speech, I said the current register is mere public relations to make the community feel better or safer.

The best moment for me and my supporters came, not in the wake of the first speech, but from an adjournment debate the following night. It was a really special moment. A feeling that 'This is what I came here for.'

That's where I broke the story about how McDonald's had been employing a convicted sex offender at a cafe inside the Panthers Football Club in Sydney and how the Penrith Baseball Club had earlier employed the man and let him umpire games that his victim was going to play in. And how it turned out that one of Australia's largest employers of young people had no policy about police checks for employees working with children.

My staff approached McDonald's on 31 August and, to Macca's credit, within twenty-four hours the sex offender had been sacked and the company had started to bring in a tougher employment code with mandatory police checks for staff over eighteen.

The size of this early political victory sunk in when a supporter texted: *You have changed the employment requirements of one of the world's largest companies. So proud and happy.*

Let's devote the rest of the diary to other first speeches.

Pauline Hanson. Despite her call for an immigration ban and herding all Muslims into the Islamic State basket—and proudly noting that her 'Asian invasion' in her speech twenty years ago had been superseded by a 'Muslim invasion'—the Hanson speech was regarded as milder than expected. I even received emails from people, not her usual supporters, saying things like 'Pauline has mellowed/matured and now more likeable.'

I got scalded on Twitter for giving her a congratulatory hug. I thought that was not an endorsement, just good manners. Unlike the Greens, who staged a noisy walkout, with leader Richard Di Natale reportedly sweeping behind the One Nation bench with a parting 'Fucking disgrace.'

That prompted a Hinch tweet: *Bad form for all 9 Greens to walk out on Hanson's First Speech. Jeez, only one Lib walked out on me and I talked for 45 minutes.*

I'm still trying to get my head around the call from One Nation's Malcolm Roberts for Australia to do a Brexit from the United Nations.

The most moving first speech came straight after Hanson's divisive effort when the Northern Territory's Malarndirri McCarthy stood behind an Aboriginal-motif lectern and talked about her Indigenous and non-Indigenous heritage.

Her direct call to Malcolm Turnbull to stop the plebiscite and not risk a hate campaign, and to remember what happened to Adam Goodes, was mind-grabbing. And then she talked about her sister, a lesbian, who ended her own personal turmoil over acceptance in her early twenties.

In the congratulatory line-up after her speech, I said, 'Yours was the one that should have gone forty-five minutes.'

THE THINGS YOU LEARN IN COMCARS

22 September 2016

ComCars: that magical, mystical, silent white fleet of taxpayer-funded, chauffeur-driven conveyors of politicians and senior judges and bureaucrats.

We learned about them in Senate School: when you can and can't use them. It seems that since former speaker Bronwyn Bishop's headline-creating Choppergate affair, things have tightened up both on the ground and in the air. And rightly so.

ComCar misuse is legendary. I remember a former house speaker airily dispatching a ComCar to ferry his mistress to the hairdresser.

Former Liberal Party leader (and speaker) Sir Billy Snedden would keep a ComCar sitting outside Melbourne restaurants for hours after yet another Melbourne thrashing when he was the Demons' number one ticket holder.

And it was a ComCar driver, with the improbable name of Les Patterson (not Sir Les of Dame Edna fame), who told me the 'hedgehog' story about Billy and the transvestite outside the drunk pollie's ex-wife's restaurant in East Melbourne.

ComCars have even made it into film, with Geraldine Turner playing an over-sexed cabinet minister in the back of one in *The Wog Boy*. Guess who that was based on?

In my first week in the Senate, I was criticised on Twitter for using a ComCar for the short trip from Parliament House to the Hyatt Canberra—despite the fact I wear a knee brace.

Apart from convenience (and that sense of entitlement), one of the reasons politicians use ComCars is for security—which is increasingly becoming an issue of office—but the risk of possible misuse is why I called an Uber to go to the movies in Canberra one weekend.

One of those short late-night shuttles to my hotel recently was long enough for a conversation that could have got my driver sacked if I were so inclined. Didn't want that, so will fudge some details in the retelling.

The first hint that this would be a different sort of ride was when the driver opened both passenger side doors for me, tossed my heavy briefcase in the back and said, 'I know you like to ride up front with me when I drive you.' It was the first time I had been in this person's car.

Once ensconced, I was told: 'Welcome. You'll discover there are two places here: Parliament House and Canberra. One of them, Canberra, is a good place.'

We had a short, bland conversation about the sheer size of the edifice carved out of a hillside and I mentioned how, in one day, I had walked 4.6 kilometres around the corridors, according to my iPhone pedometer. Then ... the zinger. 'Yeah, I was walking alone around the Senate one night and suddenly saw a man walking towards me. It was Paul Keating.

'Gee, the people you meet when you haven't got a gun!'

Welcome to Canberra, senator.

Things you learn:

Some good early advice in this rookie senatorial career was to spend as much time as possible in the chamber just watching and learning, often sitting for several hours in a near-deserted sea of red leather as Coalition and opposition senators filled the twenty minutes allotted to their parties.

It paid off in my first week when Senate president Stephen Parry allowed my first point of order against the eloquent George Brandis for evading a question.

It got me thinking. Why can't government and opposition senators ask questions of crossbenchers during question time? Why can't a Liberal senator ask a question of a constantly interjecting smart-arse like Labor senator Doug Cameron?

After all, we have to sit through all those self-serving saccharine Dorothy Dixers, to which the minister always intones stuff like 'I thank the Member for Woop Woop for the perspicacity of his question ...'

Turns out that under the Westminster system, to which we (generally) adhere, questions during question time can only be addressed to a minister or senator representing a lower house minister. Pity.

And finally …

As an old editor, I almost picked the exact tabloid headline after I realised an ex-partner had hit social media after our break-up: *Hinch on the booze again.* I did tweet HHNF—Hell hath no fury … and will finish with this explanation:

It is true that, even though the Senate dining room and the Hyatt Canberra now stock my Edenvale non-alcoholic wine, I have been known to occasionally drink real wine with the permission of my transplant surgeon, Professor Bob Jones.

SEPARATION OF CHURCH AND STATE

29 September 2016

'And no religion, too' … as John Lennon sang in his anthemic 'Imagine'.

This won't win me many friends inside or outside parliament but, in a non-sitting week for the Senate, I have a question.

Each morning that the Senate is in session, the warning bells ring four minutes before 9.30 to tell us the formalities are about to begin. We all stand like school kids at our desks as Senate president Stephen Parry walks in. He is granted judge's status with a nod of our heads, and he then leads us all in a recitation of the Lord's Prayer.

Well, not all of us. A few of the non-believers, the atheists and agnostics, like Hinch, Larissa Waters, Louise Pratt and Skye Kakoschke-Moore, stare ahead or look at the ceiling. I suspect many others, who seem to mumble their way through the prayer, took the affirmation and not the oath when they were sworn in. In fact, there weren't many Bibles being held in the right hand on 30 August.

What is the protocol? If you're not a Christian, are you meant to show respect by closing your eyes or bowing your head? Would we be showing more respect and honesty by not entering the chamber until after the prayer bit is over? But then you'd be filing in during the minute of silence that follows and the ungrammatical Welcome to Country.

Which leads to my main question: why does every session start with a recitation of a Christian prayer at all? What ever happened to separation of church and state? And if there is to be a religious start to each morning session, why not a Buddhist chant one day or a Hillsong song or a Greek Orthodox prayer?

What does Muslim MP Anne Aly do in the House of Reps, where a similar ceremony plays out? And, as Labor's Emma Husar, a Catholic, pointed out to me, it's always the Protestants' version of the Lord's Prayer that is used.

She had a good idea: why not an affirmation, like the choice we have when being sworn in or when you become a citizen?

Answers to this 'Dear Abby' quandary are welcome.

Speaking of Anne Aly, our first and only female Muslim rep in the House of Reps, we were seated together on a recent early-morning Canberra–Melbourne shuttle flight, and I witnessed what could have been an embarrassing moment. I skipped breakfast, but Aly ordered the poached eggs—which came served with bacon.

She pointed out her Muslim faith and the offending pieces of pig were removed. Then the confession: 'The only time I can say "I love bacon" is when I'm talking about my family. My family name is Bacon.'

Shutterbug update.

My campaign to give still photographers the same rights in the Senate as they have in the lower house is inching (hinching?) along.

I'm getting used to the two new buzz words in a nearly hung parliament: 'negotiate' and 'compromise'. We did that to blunt most of the cuts to the Australian Renewable Energy Agency and keep alive that futuristic project that funds research and development through the Clean Energy Finance Corporation. And I agreed to have my motion to end Senate camera censorship shunted off to a committee for review.

The committee must report back next month, and hopefully the green light will be on again. The government tells me they support it. The most vociferous Labor opponent was Stephen Conroy, and he sneaked off into the darkness (unphotographed) on the last night of the last session.

Maybe that's why when a photographer, laden with camera gear, swung open one of those heavy Senate doors for me the other day, he said, 'Do anything for you, mate.'

Indulgent quote of the week: Red Symons and his reference to 'that old guy in the Senate who looks like Derryn Hinch with young person's hair'.

BEWARE THE SENATE FASHION POLICE

6 October 2016

I was photographed at the dispatch box on the floor of the House of Reps in Old Parliament House recently, and it brought back some nostalgic memories of the prime ministers and opposition leaders I interviewed, and sometimes jousted with, on radio and television.

Including one who refused to speak to me for so long that I took the only position possible: I banned him.

In the early 1980s, Malcolm Fraser refused to come on my 3AW radio program. Maybe because I'd referred to him as that 'po-faced souvenir from the Easter Islands'.

The ban lasted for more than two years. Adding insult to injury, he appeared on almost every other program on the station. The final straw was when the PM appeared on the weekend fishing program.

For a bit of satirical fun, I took Fraser's answers from that interview and played it on my current affairs program the next day.

When he was talking about trout fishing and where the trout were jumping, I posed the question, 'Is it true that you have such a cabinet of yes men that when you say "jump", they jump?'

The PM's answer: 'Jump? They jump and jump and jump 'til they're exhausted.'

And, taking his response to a question about how few fish he'd caught last time out, I asked, 'What are you going to do for pensioners in the next budget?'

'Nothing … absolutely nothing.' And there was talk about being stranded up a creek.

The PM was not amused. The boycott/ban continued until that day in 1983 when Fraser called a snap election to catch Bill Hayden off guard—not knowing Labor was already making the switch to Bob Hawke.

We knew the election winds must be blowing against him because suddenly the prime minister dispatched an emissary to one of my lengthy Friday 'rat pack' lunches (for old journos) to call for a truce.

The white-flag carrier was the PM's media man David Barnett. The negotiated interview was flagged with full-page ads in *The Age* along the lines of 'They said it would never happen …'

I did my research, stayed off the turps, had an early night, and … Malcolm Fraser walked all over me. He filibustered, a knack he was good at. Like the old union man John Halfpenny, the PM could almost keep talking on the inhale. Hardly drew breath.

I also recall that, despite the studio being packed with TV cameras and reporters, David Barnett was quite unabashedly kneeling on the floor alongside Fraser and occasionally handed him 8×4 cards with suggested answers printed on them.

That was the day where the seed for 'Shame, shame, shame' was sown—but that's for another day.

———————

Sartorial elegance is an issue that seems to consume some people in the nation's capital. And I'm not talking about Nick Xenophon turning up in his jammies for a marathon session as a stunt.

It is not a prerequisite for a senator to wear a tie. I do. The Greens' Peter Whish-Wilson doesn't.

But another fashion decision has caused me some angst. Well, caused some confusion for other senators.

For years, I have followed the fashion, and comfort, trend of not tucking in a business or dress shirt. In the Senate, or at a desk, with a jacket buttoned up, nobody is any the wiser. But on seeing my untucked shirt, two senators (David Leyonhjelm and Nick Xenophon) have gestured to me as if my fly were undone, and a staffer for Liberal MP Ken Wyatt tried to wise me up when we had a photo op for the Transplant Games.

The best response came from a female security guard at the Senate entrance. She alerted me to the errant piece of shirt.

When I explained, 'It's called fashion,' she said, 'Well, if I were your mother, I'd give you a smack!'

She looked like she would have too.

Brings back memories of a childhood ditty I couldn't find on Google, which went:

Jimmy Jimmy Jout (?)
Your shirt's hanging out
Five miles in
And five miles out.

Or something like that.

Finally, my tweet of the week. At the Fair Work hearing on the firefighters' dispute, in Victoria's Parliament House, Greens senator Lee Rhiannon was struggling to find a vital clause in the massive enterprise bargaining agreement book. Couldn't help it: she's now *a rebel without a clause*.

GOOD RIDDANCE TO A GRUBBY PLEBISCITE

13 October 2016

Who's playing politics now over the 'P' word? It is true that Bill Shorten and Labor have shamelessly exploited the plebiscite debate leading up to the staged, but effective, Parliament House announcement that caucus had voted to block the plebiscite legislation. Hold the front page!

Their twenty-six Senate votes have been in the 'no' column for weeks. As have been nine Greens votes, three from the Xenophon Team and one from Hinch.

Thirty-nine. Enough to rightfully kill this $200 million public opinion poll, which would not lock in politicians like conservative Coalition senator Eric Abetz, who still seems to think that homosexuality or heterosexuality is a 'lifestyle'. Gimme a break.

(I'm itching for the time I can announce a plan on how to spend that $200 million on something tangible that will help thousands of Australian families. Bravehearts, I'm listening.)

We expected the plebiscite bill to hit the Senate yesterday. It didn't. And it seems it won't today, and then we break until November. This is cynically shameless behaviour from a government that has been bleating the opposition has been cruelly playing politics with gay people's lives. And their children's lives.

Bring it on. A senior cabinet minister admitted to me this week that the plebiscite fight was lost shortly after the attorney-general and government leader in the Senate, George Brandis, had appealed on the floor that there was still time for Senator Derryn Hinch to change his mind. I won't. I really hope mine is the vote that sinks this grubby backbench compromise for a public vote that both the PM and Brandis were against last year.

———

At yesterday's official Great Hall lunch for Singapore's prime minister Lee Hsien Loong, which, entertainingly, included the PM's boyhood memories of Melbourne, Bill Shorten produced an example of the sort of bipartisan camaraderie that prospers when a friendly country's leader is in town.

He said, 'Prime Minister Lee, you've created such a unity in this place that Mr Turnbull and I are wearing the same colour suits and the same colour ties.' It got a laugh.

No risk of them wearing Tony Abbott's baby-blue number.

It reminded me of a day when I was interviewing prime minister Paul Keating on the *Midday* show in the 1990s. I noticed a funny fashion coincidence. During a commercial break, I pointed out we were not only wearing identical black double-breasted Zegna suits, we also had on identical silk ties. (One of the perks of TV: after I got sacked by Channel Nine, then went broke and had my year-long Grizzly Adams period in flannel shirt and gumboots on my farm, there were still more than a dozen Zegna suits hanging in my wardrobe. Thanks, Kerry.)

Getting back to former prime minister Tony Abbott. He featured a couple of times in the Lee speech, including a yarn about a barbecue, and I thought Turnbull showed class when he beckoned Abbott to join him on the house floor for the meet-and-greet after the speeches.

Not quite so lucky was Greens leader Richard Di Natale. At the crowded leaders' table, he had to sit at a desk alone like a house stenographer and in the handshake parade he got missed on the first run-through. A mini-repeat of when Governor-General Peter Cosgrove swept past the outstretched hand of Tanya Plibersek at a special sitting of parliament.

Okay. The Hanson–Hinch televised stoush over Donald Trump.

I tried to be civilised on *Sunrise* when Hanson started defending this loathsome man. We did the Canberra TV cross in different studios and then I bumped into her in the press gallery corridor. I actually stood back so I wouldn't inter-rupt her interview. But when our paths crossed, I couldn't just pretend to all that it was sweetness and light. Not after her 'locker-room talk' and 'All men do it' defence on TV. I'd watched seven hours of Trump on CNN over the weekend and was sick of Trumpets, especially women, defending a man I accurately called a 'sexual predator'.

It was real. It was raw. I've been told my body language showed my anger.

I mentioned the Singapore PM House of Reps speech, to which senators were invited. I was told several times, 'Sit where you like.' I did. On the opposition frontbench. Whoops. Chatted with The Interrupter, Senator Doug Cameron, and then retired to the second row.

I'll finish with pronunciation (or should that now be pronounciation?).

In their justifiable denunciation of Senate leader George Brandis over his power play with the solicitor-general, both Penny Wong and Kim Carr used the word 'dis-associate'.

I dissociate myself from that.

A JOURNO'S NIGHTMARE—SCOOPS YOU CAN'T TOUCH

20 October 2016

There was a touch of James Bond in there. A solemn-faced government official knocked on my office door. The large black briefcase wasn't shackled to her wrist, but it did have a huge lock and protruding key.

She sat down and, after the doors were closed and I had deactivated my mobile phone (and iPad camera), she handed me two bulky folders.

The Interim and Final Confidential Reports, Volume 6, of the *Royal Commission into Trade Union Governance and Corruption*. The redacted interim report was more than 300 pages. The final report, about 450.

I had given a written guarantee that I would take no notes, no photographs and would not pass on what I was about to read to any third person. A breach could send me to jail. Been there, done that—too often.

I must admit, though (the journo in you never dies), that I felt a bit like Laurie Oakes when he had that federal budget dropped in his lap.

The difference was, I had a scoop I could never use.

Jacqui Lambie, who had also read it, told us it would only take an hour. Maybe she skipped all the big words. It took me 2-and-a-half hours, and the government minder did not leave my side.

In the interim report, about twenty consecutive pages were redacted and, from what preceded them and followed, they were obviously censored because of upcoming court cases.

Some names and addresses were also blacked out—presumably because there were fears for some witnesses' safety and their families' safety. And that's all I am going to say about it.

———

I've now been a senator for seven weeks. As I pointed out on *Sunrise* on Monday, that morning was a year to the day since I launched my Don Quixote quest in the form of the Justice Party.

Judging by some Facebook and Twitter comments, I've been an abject failure because I haven't already cured cancer, reformed the Family Court, cleaned up child welfare agencies nationwide and brought about peace in the Middle East.

Immodestly, I'll quote seasoned advisers on my staff who claim I've achieved more in seven weeks than some party hacks achieve in seven years.

We overturned the photo ban in the Senate, an anachronistic, misguided, protection of senators' privacy, which had been fought by the press gallery for twenty-five years. It ends next month.

McDonald's is changing its employment policy to protect teenage employees from convicted sex offenders.

We are working to force states to tighten their Working With Children permits. As I said in the Senate the other night, you can start working with vulnerable kids the minute you produce your post office receipt for lodging an application, even though approval may take six to eight weeks. Noddyland.

And we are making huge progress in getting the passports of convicted Australian paedophiles who still go on child rape holidays in Cambodia, Malaysia, Thailand, Myanmar, Indonesia and the Philippines cancelled. It will happen.

———

The Greens this week produced a social media report showing who voted against them. I figured high in the 'no' column. I've told some of them we should make a political movie called *A Bridge Too Far* because, I am realising, the Greens are classic overreachers. Maybe that's a minor-party trait.

I don't hate the Greens. I love their push for transparency. That's why I have voted several times with them to send issues to committee.

I am actually working on co-sponsoring with Lee Rhiannon a bill on banning live exports, and Rachel Siewert is a hard-working gem.

So, why a bridge too far? Because of a ritual. I'll sit down with my advisers and start going through the Greens' latest proposed bill. Looks good. 'Just common sense,' as we campaigned on.

Clause 1, clause 2, I can live with that. Clause 3 is a 'maybe', but then clause 4 is really that overreaching 'pixies at the bottom of the garden' stuff that Paul Keating used to accuse the Australian Democrats of.

It's sad, because their hearts are in the right place.

And now to go back to a time that many readers won't even remember. A time when news photos were transmitted from 'picturegram trucks', and by 'facsimile' before it became known as a 'fax machine'.

The memory-lane stroll was triggered by the death of the world's longest-reigning monarch, King Bhumibol of Thailand.

The king and his exquisite regal consort, Queen Sirikit, visited Australia in 1962.

One photo that sputtered out of the facsimile machine at that time stayed on reporters' smoke-stained walls for years. Not because of the picture but because of the savage political caption on it.

The photo showed the young Thai king Bhumibol on the left and the porcelain Sirikit on the right. In the middle was the prime minister, Robert Menzies.

The caption: 'A c— between two Thais'.

I remember it vividly, more than fifty years later.

SEXIST, PATRONISING AND STUPID

27 October 2016

Any reader within cooee of my age group may remember that Monty Python classic sketch 'Argument Clinic'. The one where Michael Palin walks into an office and says, 'I'd like to have an argument, please.' And then he gets into a scrap with the receptionist over whether he wants to pay one pound for a five-minute argument or eight pounds for a course of ten.

By mistake, he walks into the 'Abuse' course and is told: 'You snotty-faced heap of parrot droppings. You vacuous toffee-nosed malodorous pervert. Shut your festering gob, you tit. Your type makes me puke.'

Would it surprise you if I said that savage satire came to mind last week when the novice senator had his first taste of Senate estimates committee hearings?

They are long, they are savage and, at times, demeaning of the government ministers and department heads who are hauled in for marathon Q and A sessions with opposition senators—and the dreaded crossbenchers.

Some politicians have made themselves fearsome reputations from their relentless grilling of ministers and public servants. The forensic John Faulkner was one. Bronwyn Bishop was another.

The most thorough and indefatigable combatant last week was the militant Doug Cameron, who showed amazing stamina by being there from the opening bat until stumps. Showing the same stamina were committee chairmen/women who some days held court from 9 a.m. until 11 p.m.

Rudest were senators Barry O'Sullivan and Ian Macdonald. Best line was from a session I was sitting in on when Penny Wong asked attorney-general George Brandis, 'Would you just like to be pompous for the whole day, or only for this question?'

But it was Macdonald, the so-called 'Father of the Senate', who shocked me at a private corridor huddle of senators and a Senate clerk's office official, as a procedural matter was thrashed out that same day.

As a newbie, and accepting this was a confidential senatorial stoush, I shan't repeat the conversation but, if I were asked to categorise Macdonald's demeanour and attitude to the Senate opposition leader, I would have trouble excluding words like 'patronising', 'sexist' and—as Monty Python would say—'vacuous' and 'toffee-nosed'.

———

At Senator Jacqui Lambie's suggestion, I have not applied to join many permanent Senate committees. Instead, I'll remain a participating senator with the right to drop in on any committee and interrogate any witness. I won't get a vote on a final report, but I can file a dissenting opinion.

Interesting that committee chairs for estimates are told they have the same powers as the Senate president, can order a session to be held in camera and can chastise bad behaviour. Macdonald didn't rebuke himself. He should have.

———————

Speaking of senators behaving badly … David Leyonhjelm is one of the most intelligent people in that chamber. One of the most intelligent—and most stupid.

I said on *Sunrise* that I find it reprehensible, unconscionable, for an elected member of parliament to say he would be happy for police 'to lie on the side of the road and bleed to death'.

Personally, I would even go to the assistance of a bikie or a paedophile.

I'll give you an example this week of why the senator is so out of whack with genuine, community-minded Australians.

I posted a brief comment on my Justice Party Facebook page on Saturday about a chance coffee-shop meeting with a uniformed policeman who was upset because an ice-addicted man from Afghanistan named Fawad Aroofi, twenty-eight, had not been sentenced to even one day in jail after an incident outside a McDonald's where he deliberately crashed into a police car and an ambulance, and ran over a police officer, breaking his ribs and causing other lasting injuries.

That post, Senator Leyonhjelm, reached nearly 1.3 million people in four days. I doubt any would agree with your callous scenario.

———————

As a journo for more than fifty years, and as a former metropolitan newspaper editor, I am well aware of the word 'furphy'. Many a time has an abjectly disappointed scribe phoned in after chasing the scoop of the year to say, 'Sorry, it was a furphy.'

I've had to explain the word's origin to some young staffers because two floors above my Senate office in Canberra, at the start of the press gallery corridor, is the cast-iron rear end of a Furphy water wagon. Like the horse-drawn ones at Gallipoli—the place where soldiers whispered rumours that often turned out to be wrong. Turned out to be 'furphies'.

The relic used to be in the press gallery at Old Parliament House. This week I was shown around the former Furphy foundry, and now stainless steel tank factory, by Adam Furphy, whose dad presented that giant plaque to the press gallery.

At SPC Ardmona and at Furphy, we covered more than 4.3 kilometres of factory floors as I started to make good on an election promise to visit country towns, and meet the locals and listen to their problems—a few weeks after an election, not a desperate, vote-seeking few weeks before.

AND THEY'RE RACING ...

3 November 2016

It's Melbourne Cup Week, and the Senate doesn't sit again until next Monday, so let's start with a Cup story—prompted by Gina Rinehart's unfortunate, and unseemly, tumble down the stairs when exiting the Emirates marquee.

In her defence, if there are any snickers about John Kerr or a 'tired and emotional' state, I'll admit I held the guard rail while descending because those temporary stairs were steep, deceptive and tricky. And I was drinking non-alcoholic wine I'd had couriered in.

The Rinehart incident reminded me of a similar tumble in the members' enclosure in the early 1980s. The Cup's indomitable fashion doyenne, Lillian Frank, fell to the bottom of a stalled escalator, just outside the champagne bar. As she lay on the ground, with a badly gashed leg and another flamboyant headpiece knocked askew, comedian Doug Mulray was heard to shout, 'Put a screen around her and shoot her!' I was standing alongside of him. I think he was joking.

(It was good to see Lillian, and peripatetic party-goer husband Richard, back at Emirates on Tuesday.)

———————

Speaking of the new commendably lite version of the Rinehart—who I'm told can't be described as an heiress anymore because she inherited mainly debt from Lang—it was, surprisingly, the first time we had ever met. A pleasant conversation followed, in which she said, 'We'd better not talk too long or people will think we're discussing Kidman.' I said, 'We'll tell them we are … talking about Nicole.'

———————

And on the subject of meeting people for the first time, at Mumm's marquee I met Chloe Shorten and had a good chat about some of the issues that got me elected. Is it uncharitable to surmise that Bill is batting out of his crease—as they used to say of Julia Gillard's mate, old what'sisname?

———————

Further to those issues—like my push for a national public register of convicted sex offenders—I caught up with actress Rachel Griffiths, whom I've known since she was a teenager.

A worldwind (deliberate new word) of talent, she was at Flemington, directing *Ride Like a Girl*, her new movie about 2015 Melbourne Cup winner Michelle Payne.

We were talking about vile sex offenders in such an incongruous setting because, minutes before I gave a Melbourne Press Club speech recently, a hastily scrawled note from Rachel was thrust into my hand.

I knew she had been quietly campaigning for years against Australian men going on what I call 'child rape holidays' in Cambodia. In her note, which I read aloud that day, she made the chilling point that a bankrupt Australian can have his passport suspended and overseas trips banned for seven years but convicted paedophiles are free to travel.

It was the spark I needed to raise that issue in my first speech. Since then, I have met with foreign minister Julie Bishop, immigration minister Peter Dutton, Border Force chiefs and the Australian Federal Police. Encouragingly, at a recent meeting of state and federal justice and police ministers in Melbourne, they agreed to form a working group to see what could be accomplished.

The group is to report back next year. I think something can be done sooner without new legislation and 'in the national interest' by invoking current regulations. About 200 sleazebags have gone on such holidays in the past two years to Cambodia, Malaysia, Thailand, Myanmar, Indonesia and the Philippines.

Not coincidentally, last night I spoke at an anti-human slavery and child exploitation fundraiser in Sydney. Interestingly, Anti-Slavery Australia, based at the University of Technology in Sydney, is, I believe, the only university-based research centre in Australia dedicated to the rights of people who have experienced human trafficking here and abroad. And it does happen here. Think of Muslim child brides.

What was encouraging at the races was the number of young women, many of them young mothers (inexplicably wanting selfies), who, even in a carnival atmosphere, wanted to talk about the sex offender register and offer support for what we're trying to achieve in Canberra. They were aware of the changes we forced on McDonald's staff screening procedures, and the call for a passport ban.

———

Almost forgot. David Leyonhjelm took to Twitter late Saturday night to steal a line from my last *Crikey* column and call me a 'dumb pile of parrot droppings'—or something like that: *@HumanHeadline You need to read this and apologise to me, you dumb heap of parrot droppings.*

He demanded an apology for something I'd written. I declined. Stuck to my Twitter law: answer a tweet once, personally or generally, then disengage. At least he reads my Twitter.

WHY I'LL VOTE TO REPEAL 18C

10 November 2016

About twenty-five years ago, I wrote a best-selling book called *The Derryn Hinch Diet.*

It was a soup and wine diet. Dinner consisted of soup, a bread roll and white wine. We joked that you'd heard of the Fit for Life diet? This was the Pissed for Life diet. Sounded really witty before I needed a liver transplant to stay alive.

The diet worked, and it got a healthy heart tick. The book climbed to number one on the Sydney *Daily Telegraph* best-seller list—even ahead of Naomi Wolf and *The Beauty Myth.*

Soup, alphabet soup, was on my mind this week as we headed back into Canberra for the final three weeks of Senate sittings for 2016.

I said to Prime Minister Turnbull at a green tea and chat meeting that I was consumed by a soup of letters and numbers: ABCC, PPL, 18C.

In the next three weeks, I'm going to have to vote on all of them (unless the Australian Building and Construction Commission is again put in the too-hard basket). A couple of us crossbenchers have already flagged amendments to the first two, which the beleaguered government seems amenable to. The 'hate speech' bill, with apparent prime ministerial blessing, is headed for a joint committee scrutiny. Removal of 'offend' and 'insult' is my fallback position, but I'd scrap 18C from the *Racial Discrimination Act* completely if I had my 'druthers', as the Americans would say.

(Trivial Pursuit question: what does 'druthers' mean? It's a slangy truncation of 'I would rather.' See, the stuff you learn here …)

––––––––––

When the Senate decided to send the fates of senators Bob Day and Rod Culleton off to the High Court (sitting as the Court of Disputed Returns), I decided it was an opportunity to raise an issue that should never be an election issue: the exclusion from our Senate or House of Representatives of any person who carries dual citizenship at the time of their election.

It is clearly stated in the constitution that failure to renounce allegiance to another country, another power, makes a person ineligible to hold office. I realise that by even raising the issue I risk reigniting the so-called 'Australian birther movement' surrounding the eligibility of former prime minister Tony Abbott and when he officially renounced his British citizenship. So be it. My notice of motion is aimed at all members of parliament, current and future.

The Member for Warringah could have killed that issue—and headed off that 40 000-strong petition—by pulling his renunciation document out of his bottom drawer (where I store my revocation certificate from New Zealand), rather than having the PM's office seal the document with a confidentiality stamp.

It surprised me that any dual citizen was not required to produce that cancellation proof before nominations closed. One of the Justice Party candidates renounced both British and Swiss citizenship before that deadline.

The 18C prosecution of Queensland students over Facebook posts was a disgrace. And so much for freedom of speech. The sanctioned persecution of Bill Leak is only surpassed by the milquetoasts who signed letters and ads of support for his official tormentors. As I said on Sky News: '*Je suis* Charlie— but bugger Bill Leak.'

Imagine if I'd voted in favour of the same-sex marriage plebiscite? I received a letter from a disgruntled constituent. She called me a 'poor excuse for a human being', hoped the karma train would hit me, hoped most of my kids and grandchildren would become gay and I would be doing the world a favour if I just 'buggered off'. The writer said she had a daughter and a nephew, of whom she was proud, who were gay and hoped I would end up in an aged care facility being cared for by a gay person.

My response:

And proud you should be. I am shocked and mystified by your vile email. I voted against the plebiscite with the support of so many gay and lesbian and bisexual groups who feared a hateful plebiscite campaign. Just today, a group of gay people and their parents awarded me a poster on the Senate lawn as a Thank You for opposing the plebiscite. My hope, like other senators who voted it down last night, is that we get a free vote and—as I said in the Senate last night— we could have legal gay marriages by Xmas.

   And if your prediction comes true, and I do end up in a nursing home, I would be thrilled to have a gay aide look after me. DH

———————

Did I say that? In question time, Senator George Brandis leaves out a word: 'The people of Australia expect nothing of us.' He meant to say, 'expect nothing less'.

AN EX-CON IN THE SENATE

17 November 2016

It's called the voice of experience. It was heard in the middle of a typically terse Senate exchange one morning, between Greens senator Nick McKim and attorney-general George Brandis, acting as the PM's rep in the Senate.

   They were debating the Counter-Terrorism Legislation Amendment Bill (No. 1) 2016 and had got into verbal ping-pong about a clause involving a person wearing an electronic tracking device having to report a faulty device within four hours.

As usual, McKim was throwing in some hypotheticals, until he squeezed a concession from the A-G that, of course, they would look sympathetically at a situation if a man were only fifteen minutes late.

It was sort of the bland leading the blind. I thought it was time for my voice of experience:

> Mr Chairman, as probably the only person in this chamber who has ever worn an electronic tracking device—for five months—let me try to explain to you that the person probably would not know that their tracking device was not working.
>
> The tracking device is monitored by a gadget in your house, but it is the people who are monitoring the tracking device who will know that it is not working—because there is movement by you and the device is not showing where you are going or what you are doing.
>
> The Attorney-General is not quite right when he talks about trivial matters—like four hours being four hours and fifteen minutes—because I was escorted down to the Justice Department when I was back late from a one-hour, doctor-approved, exercise time in my courtyard. Walking around, like Rudolf Hess, the last prisoner in Spandau jail.
>
> I was twenty-eight seconds late back, according to my device, and was threatened with being incarcerated for being in breach. So, when you are talking about it being four hours, or five hours or whatever it is, it will be the people at the other end,

the officials, who will decide. It will be the AFP, if that is the case, who will say: 'This device is not working; we must do something about it.'

See, it's good to have an ex-con on hand to fill in the details.

———————

This week, the Senate Legal and Constitutional Affairs Committee held a public hearing in Melbourne and dealt mainly with submissions and evidence about Manus and Nauru. The session carried even more import because of the PM's announcement of a deal for the US to take a (still unspecified) number of refugees off both islands. And because the US had just elected Donald Trump with all his anti-Muslim, anti-migrant campaign rhetoric.

As I asked on Twitter: *Refugee question: how does Aust. Govt. convince any foreign Govt. (with own problems) to take refugees that we won't?*

I followed it up at the hearing by asking immigration and border protection department secretary Michael Pezzullo what was the quid pro quo?

We know the payback for sending five or six refugees to Cambodia was $55 million. So, what was it with Uncle Sam? We take a few of theirs from Costa Rica? Allow 10 000 more Marines into Darwin? Expand Pine Gap?

Mr Secretary assured me it was none of the above. And I'm sure he also told me that 'under our arrangement' such deals for more action in Darwin or Pine Gap wouldn't be necessary.

———————

A senatorial exchange at that hearing prompted this tweet: *They want my vote? Senator Macdonald accuses me of asking Dorothy Dixers at Senate Nauru/Manus committee inquiry today.*

Last Friday was one of the proudest days of my short political career. I was able to hold a press conference and issue a media release about a ban on passports for convicted paedophiles, to stop them going on child rape holidays to places like Cambodia, Myanmar, Malaysia, Vietnam, Thailand, the Philippines and, of course, Indonesia.

Cynics asked (there's that quid pro quo again) if I'd done an ABCC deal with the government. Not true. PM Turnbull, foreign minister Julie Bishop and justice minister Michael Keenan were as repulsed as I was by these vile vacations.

The Federal Police told me that last year 800 convicted sex offenders went overseas, more than 300 of them to South-East Asia.

In a weekly wind-down in my Senate office, we've started holding a political quiz hosted by political adviser Sarah Mennie. I call her 'Official Occasion'. (Run her names together and you may get it.)

One question last Friday stumped many: 'What is Malcolm Turnbull's middle name?' If I said there was a bounty on it, you might come up with the correct answer: Bligh.

It reminded me of a great pub trivia middle-name question. What was President Harry S Truman's middle name? I'll give you a clue. Ask yourself why there's no full stop after the S. Because former haberdasher Harry Truman didn't have a middle name. He was told that all presidents had to have one—FDR (and later JFK and LBJ). So, Harry just took the letter S. No name, just 'S'. I always liked 'Robert James Lee Hawke' and 'Jeffrey Gibb Kennett'. Store them away for pub trivia nights.

BEWARE THE GANG OF FOUR

24 November 2016

It was actually quite bizarre. Almost surreal. The Hinch transformation. The journo turned politician.

There I was, only a few years ago, railing on Melbourne's 3AW and on TV about Craig Thomson. The former union official (and Gillard government balance-of-power holder) who had used his Health Services Union members' money for $500 hookers.

To make it more surreal, between those editorial attacks on Thomson, I had been lying in a bed at the Austin Hospital. And one day I saw one of his union members—probably earning $15 an hour—mopping up the muck from a burst colostomy bag. I thought, 'That middle-aged European woman's annual union fees probably paid for one of Thomson's union-funded assignations.'

And here I was this week: Senator Hinch, moving an auditor control amendment to a piece of government industrial relations legislation that—if it had existed when the Thomsons and Kathy Jacksons and Michael Williamsons were running the HSU—could have saved millions of dollars.

Who would have thunk it?

It was an amendment of which I was proud. Almost as proud as I was of the amendment that Nick Xenophon (and his NXT trio) and I negotiated with employment minister Michaelia Cash for one of the best whistleblower protection laws in the world.

Right now it hits union whistleblowers. Soon it will protect corporate whistleblowers. In the Senate debate I quoted my grandma: 'What's sauce for the goose is sauce for the gander.'

And to those critics who derided Nick X and me for trusting the government over future whistleblower legislation to include corporate Australia—like banks and insurance companies and the Australian Defence Froce—let me say, if you don't trust them, trust us.

The new Hinch–Team X liaison is a new Gang of Four. We don't agree on everything (and my cynical-journalist background prepares me for Greeks bearing gifts), but we suddenly have a government genuinely talking to, listening to and negotiating with the crossbench. Can't be a bad thing.

———————

This week, I delivered one of the most important speeches in the Senate that I ever will. It concerns a medical scandal involving Australian mothers that many, if not most, of you won't have even heard of.

I likened it to the Thalidomide scandal back in the 1950s and 1960s, when women who were innocently taking a morning sickness pill started giving birth to babies with no arms or legs.

Drugs like Distaval were taken off the market and a shocked world asked how could it have gone on so long? How could the drug companies in Australia have known for so many months and put so many pregnancies at risk? How could they put money before morality? Profit before pain?

How could our medical authorities and health protection agencies have been so ignorant? Or complacent?

Thalidomide became a dirty word. This week I put another word into that category: 'mesh'. Transvaginal mesh. It is not crippling babies but has crippled thousands of mothers both here and overseas.

And once again, the drug companies and the so-called watchdogs like the TGA—the Therapeutic Goods Administration—are letting victims down.

For about twenty years, this plastic (or polypropylene) mesh has been permanently embedded as post-natal hammocks, slings and netting, for prolapsed organs and incontinence (a miracle treatment for male incontinence too, I've been told).

Over time, this 'harmless' plastic netting can become brittle and start to break away in shards and splinters. These start to float around the body, causing inflammation and excruciating pain. No wonder these slings have been called 'a torture device'.

There have been cases where a splinter has pierced a woman's vaginal wall and injured her partner during intercourse.

I have read case histories and about some of the side effects: infection, bleeding, painful sexual intercourse, vaginal scarring, prolapse return, sepsis, immune system rejection, urinary problems, chronic pain. And the pain of daily living. Stabbing pain when sitting on the toilet, when crawling into bed, walking, sitting at a desk …

It just goes on. And on. It is a national disgrace.

I was not exaggerating when I linked transvaginal mesh to Thalidomide. This is one of the greatest medical scandals and abuses of mothers in our history. And I fervently believe a Senate inquiry is a must. We have to do it.

One of the banes and bugbears of a new senator's life is question time. It should be called answer time but, on reflection, that wouldn't be accurate. Ministers rarely answer questions.

To make it worse, even senators asking Dorothy Dixers get a question and two supplementary ones.

My patience was stretched this week when Victorian senator James Paterson lobbed a lollipop to Michaelia Cash about the virtues of the ABCC. This was in the midst of protracted debate from both sides on the controversial industrial relations legislation.

'Can the minister inform the Senate of the need to reform the workplace culture in the building and construction industry?'

Rising on a point of order, I said, 'Mr President, it may be my ignorance, but is it form for question time to be used to debate issues that are already in legislation before the Senate?'

The president: 'Thank you, Senator Hinch. The question is certainly in order, and I call the minister. Sit down, please.'

―――――

Pot calling kettle? Overheard from a Senator Malcolm Roberts staffer discussing the beleaguered Senator Rod Culleton, 'He's got to stop with the conspiracy theories.'

BACKPACKERS AND BACKSTABBING

1 December 2016

The colourful ghost of legendary Labor pollie Fred Daly lurked in the Senate corridors yesterday. But I was obviously showing my age as callow journos looked at me askance ('Fred who?') when I invoked one of his most famous quotes. The old raconteur once described political fame thus: 'You're a rooster one day, a feather duster the next.'

In my case, it didn't take a day. More like ten minutes. And my rapid decline in stature was only in the eyes of government ministers. Senator Hinch was being congratulated for a raft of amendments (some of which had been endorsed by opposition Senate leader Penny Wong) as the ABCC finally got across the line. Thanks to the crossbenchers—and some genuine governmental concessions—prime minister Malcolm Turnbull finally had his Christmas present.

The backslapping was brief. Within minutes, they brought on the backpacker tax. After initially backing the government's 19 per cent and then flirting with 15 per cent, I voted for Labor's, the Greens' and Jacqui Lambie's 10.5 per cent. And it was successful.

The fact was that the 10.5 per centers always started with thirty-six votes (Labor, Greens, Lambie), and with only thirty-six voters guaranteed (Libs + Nats = 30, Xenophon = 3, Hanson = 3), the government was always in trouble. My vote wouldn't have got them there, because Senator David Leyonhjelm was agin 'em and they'd miscounted Senator Rod Culleton, who was never in their bag. And there was the now magic opposition thirty-eight. If I had voted with the government, they would still have lost.

I stood by what I said at a media conference the day before: 'Let's get the bloody thing over.' Go with a proven winner. The government was more than peeved. One Liberal senator shirt-fronted me in the lobby with 'But I thought you were on our side?'

After the vote, I had my first experience of the 'full court press', with visits or phone calls from the PM, Scott Morrison, Mathias Cormann, and several corridor skirmishes.

ScoMo held a press conference saying he was still confident of passing a 15 per cent version of the bill, as I was telling journos that claims I would back it were 'bullshit'.

As I walked into the PM's office that morning, I greeted him with 'Another day in paradise …' The irony was not lost on him.

———————

This week ABCC became a four-letter word. For some, it was ever thus. I said in the Senate:

> As I was about to board the flight to Canberra on Sunday afternoon I received a text from an old Canberra hand—as they used to call them— warning me to brace myself because it was going to be 'a very nasty week'. I'd already had a taste of it over the weekend as the debate over the looming Senate brawl played out on Twitter and other social media. There was a charming tweet directed at me showing a picture of a pair of blood-stained hands.

I also said the 'Twitter sheep' probably hadn't read the legislation, let alone the huge amount of groundbreaking amendments that I managed to get the government to accept. And mightily helped along by other crossbenchers Nick Xenophon and a brave Rod Culleton (breaking away from One Nation).

I won't go into them all again here, but we managed to get a Labor amendment about Aussie workers and 457 visas included, and Penny Wong pulled a couple of amendments after I amended mine on retrospectivity.

That's why I could honestly say the bill that passed can and should work for the benefit of workers and employers, and work against the thugs and goons and liars and cheats on both sides.

———————

I can see why newbies in Canberra reportedly put on 7 kilograms in their first year. I haven't (yet), probably because of a daily grabbed chicken caesar salad from Aussie's Cafe and walking about 5–6 kilometres a day around the building. Plus, a new commitment to the bandanna-ed Peter Fitz's ban on sugar.

But all that goes out the window on a marathon sitting day like the ABCC one this week.

Capital Hill's food guru and TV journalist Annabel Crabb scored a culinary photo scoop with a pic of a junk food dispenser showing every rack for potato chips as bare as Mother Hubbard's cupboard.

I do know that Michaelia Cash had a Snickers bar for dinner and I had a Picnic bar and a Carman's muesli bar. Why? Because the Australian Food and Grocery Council scored an unwitting PR coup.

They chose that day to deliver Christmas boxes of Aussie sweet treats to all our offices. They were swooped on like a seagull swoops on a hot chip.

Do they have to be declared on the pecuniary interests register? Consider them declared.

HINCH IN CFMEU'S POCKET?

5 December 2016

On the second-last day of the year for the 45th parliament, this newly elected senator made a mistake. I'll admit the novice politician blundered over the backpackers tax.

When the government moved to reduce it from 20 per cent to 15 per cent, I should have voted with them. They didn't have the numbers (because senators David Leyonhjelm and Rod Culleton had deserted them) and they would have lost even with my vote.

But my final forty-eight hours of the sitting year would have been far more tranquil if I had voted with the government—having supported them at 19 per cent—and gone down with the ship. Then, as I have since told the PM, it would have been their problem to solve and I could have stayed under the radar, still basking in the accolades for supporting the ABCC legislation that had triggered the double dissolution. Albeit supporting it with tough, controversial amendments.

Instead, I took that Canberra buzz word 'compromise' too seriously. On the floor of the Senate, I suddenly saw the cause was lost and decided instead to vote with those supporting 10.5 per cent, which I knew could get passed, the fruit and flowers could be picked, and we could all go home with a Christmas present.

I said at a media conference that I didn't care if it was 10 per cent or 15 per cent. Just get the bleeping thing done.

I've lost some skin over this. It was the most pressure-packed week I have had in my entire life. I'm learning. Starting to believe that whatever doesn't kill you makes you stronger. At least they all know I will not horse trade.

On the last *Insiders* for the year, Nick Xenophon said I should be cut some slack as the new pollie on the block and I would learn.

As I tweeted: Nick X. I guess that means I learn to horse trade like you did on water and Leyonhjelm on 15%. Hope I'm a slow learner.

I copped it from all sides after the ABCC legislation got passed with my vote—again, after a swag of Hinch-demanded amendments. Most of it was along the lines that the novice had been hoodwinked by the CFMEU or they had bought me a holiday house or financed my re-election campaign. Not true. Didn't even buy me a (non-alcoholic) beer.

I even refused to meet with any union bosses in Canberra last week.

The biggest canard being regurgitated by heaps of 'expert' commentators was that I had sold out by including a two-year transition period. That figure came from the pen of the PM on a piece of paper that Senator Michaelia Cash then came into his office to witness us both signing.

The best thing I can do now is to pass on the letter I sent to *The Australian* on Friday after veteran financial commentator Bob Gottliebsen's fanciful piece. A letter they have not published. I said:

> I have known Robert Gottliebsen for more than 35 years and have admired him, worked with him and enjoyed his financial commentary. But his piece about 'Union boss outwits Hinch' (*Australian* 2.12.) is arrant nonsense.
>
> I negotiated with Michaelia Cash over the ABCC for two months and with the prime minister personally this week. They accepted some great amendments including, reluctantly, one which had Labor's imprimatur on 457 visas. It is a good piece

of industrial law. Especially for the subbies over disputed and delayed payments.

My stumbling block was always retrospectivity. I don't like retrospective laws. The government wanted to make the compliance date from April, 2014, when all they had was draft legislation which was then twice voted down in the Senate. I refused.

My argument was that EBAs [Enterprise Bargaining Agreements] negotiated before the new law gained Royal assent should stand, as in any other contract.

When they expired, all new ones had to be code compliant and no rollovers would be allowed.

Minister Cash brought a proposal to me that would give developers—wanting to apply for government contracts worth more than $100 million—nine months 'transition' to get their house in order, including apprenticeship programs etc. As well as EBAs.

That did not satisfy my demand for no retrospectivity.

At a private meeting between just me and the prime minister he suggested two years. Not me. (So, I suppose Noonan outwitted him too.) And the sinister November 29, 2018, date wasn't Noonan's—it was Turnbull's.

When I accepted several hours later, I likened it to the Paid Parental Leave bargaining. The government wanted to bring that in on January 1, 2017. I'm holding out for October 1—so it won't affect women already pregnant. Likewise, EBAs signed in 2014 would expire in 2016 or 2017. I knew Lend Lease and the CFMEU got cute and signed some expensive new agreements in 2016 but they will be crunched in 2018.

When David Noonan 'strode into Parliament House this week', as Bob Gott put it, he wasn't coming to meet me. Forget the 'gatekeeper': I refused to see him.

Right now, the unions hate some amendments to the ABCC and the bosses hate others. We must have got something right.

Senator Derryn Hinch
Melbourne

I've hosted live TV shows, anchored the Hawke–Peacock election coverage from Canberra, in a marathon seven-hour cliffhanger, and edited a metropolitan newspaper with crunch deadlines, but that was the most pressure-packed week in my entire life.

THE LONGER YOU LIVE, THE SOONER YOU DIE

15 December 2016

In this, my last Senate diary jottings for 2016, I must keep one figure in mind. That number is 6 039 000. That's the most recent statistic for the population of the state of Victoria. The state I represent in Canberra.

It's a timely reminder that, although nearly a quarter of a million Victorians gave me their primary Senate vote, millions didn't.

And I sit on that red leather bench representing the rights and welfare of all those people.

Actually, I think we have done well in the less than four months I have been a Victorian senator. And this will not be a campaign speech.

I'll just say we have got McDonald's, one of Australia's biggest employers, to change its policy on hiring convicted sex offenders—after we found one at the Penrith Panthers McDonald's outlet offering teenage employees a ride home after a late finish.

There was government backing for my campaign to pull the passports of convicted paedophiles going on child rape holidays in South-East Asia. I was alerted to this issue by actress Rachel Griffiths, who asked how come a person judged to be bankrupt has their passport confiscated for seven years but the same doesn't apply to a criminal on the sex offender register.

I found out from the Federal Police that 800 convicted sex offenders went overseas last year and more than 300 of them went to places like Cambodia, Thailand, Myanmar and Malaysia.

Nick Xenophon and I got some major whistleblower protection issues embedded in government legislation, plus greater scrutiny of 457 visa rorts, and protection of subbies' payments.

Getting photographers in the Senate the right to click away and do their jobs was a media freedom success—after the ban on it had been in place for decades.

My main goals for next year are: to continue working with the states on a national public register of convicted sex offenders; and to have a Senate committee investigation, with public hearings, into a medical scandal, which I have described as the biggest involving Australian women since the Thalidomide tragedy of the 1950s and 1960s. That is, the continued implantation of transvaginal mesh into women suffering from incontinence and prolapse problems. The mesh, which degrades in the human body, has been banned in Scotland, is under review in Canada, and is the subject of lawsuits involving 100 000 women in the United States.

I am also sitting on a new Senate committee—along with David Leyonhjelm and Sam Dastyari. It's aimed at slashing red tape in this country, in government agencies and private industry.

———————

Speaking of Senator Sam, he's been back in the news. Back where he knows he belongs—except when holding train-wreck press conferences about his China plates. He's in the news because, rumour has it, he has served his penance over bill-paying malfeasance and will be back on the opposition frontbench when we resume in February.

The self-proclaimed Dasher also featured recently in one of the strangest discussions of hirsuteness that I heard on the Senate floor. And, to a newcomer, there were some trivial doozies.

Dasher said:

> … I note that when I asked my second question of Senator Brandis today, he could barely be heard over the jeers that were coming from the other side of the chamber in what was nothing more than a relentless and unfair attack on my hairstyle. Let me be clear: we cannot all be as fortunate as Senator Hinch, who is in this chamber today. We may all try

to aspire to have what Senator Hinch has, but none of us can be that fortunate and none of us can be that lucky.

It can be a hair-raising place.

A hangover from prohibition? Being a newbie has given me the perfect solution to the annual Christmas present quandary, in the shape of the Senate gift shop near the front door, which has for sale embossed Senate mugs, cufflinks, wineglasses and pens.

One great souvenir, I thought, was a small bottle of 'Parliament House gin' for a friend in the United States. It boomeranged from Australia Post, with an official letter pointing out that 'alcohol (gin) is a prohibited import into the USA'.

And I hope I have heard for the last time from a cheery flight attendant 'You must be enjoying your holidays,' as we fly back into Canberra yet again. Just because parliament isn't sitting until February, that doesn't mean you are not working, at estimates committee meetings.

And then there are the emails and calls from heaps of the frustrated and angry and hurting among those 6 039 000 constituents. And the woman in Queensland complaining about the poor condition of 'speckled fruit' in her local supermarket. Even sent me a photo to prove it. I know how she feels. I was having the same problem with online lemons from Woolies.

So, have a safe and meaningful Yuletide season. Make the most of it. Remember the Irish saying, 'The longer you live, the sooner you die.'

And as they say (and sing) in Hawaii, 'Mele kalikimaka'.

BACK TO SCHOOL, BACK TO BUSINESS

9 February 2017

On the lush lakeside lawn at Yarralumla (my first-ever visit there, surprisingly) for the governor-general's 'back to school' soiree on Sunday night, the PM asked after my wellbeing.

I said: 'It's Groundhog Day. We left here in December talking about same-sex marriage and Cory Bernardi and here we are back in town talking about … same-sex marriage and Cory Bernardi.'

Game on, again.

Speaking of the man, who is trying to be the biggest party-wrecker with that first name since 16-year-old Corey Worthington threw a house-wrecking party at his parents' Melbourne home, Senator Bernardi was the reason I was cautioned by acting deputy Senate president Peter Whish-Wilson for unseemly language.

We'd only been back for about thirty-five minutes, on our first sitting day for 2017.

I said, 'To hear him stand there talking about principle, after he stood as a Liberal candidate and was elected by the people of South Australia as a Liberal candidate, is a joke.'

And then I made the mistake of quoting one of President Lyndon Johnson's famous crudities, when he once said about a critic of his party—and the government knows the ones they have inside their tent—on why he had not fired or tried to expel him, 'I'd rather have him inside the tent pissing out than outside the tent pissing in.'

Contrary to most commentators and their 'Another Turnbull Disaster' skew, I said, 'Maybe Malcolm Turnbull is well rid of Senator Bernardi, because at least he is now out there pissing all over everybody else, and inside his own party room he has one less ...'

The Protocol Police, Whish-Wilson, cut in with: 'Senator Hinch, I draw your attention to the standing orders. You are sailing fairly close to the wind in the use of your language.'

According to Hansard, Senator Hinch replied, 'I will take it back, but I will leave the quote from President Johnson, because he is a President and he said it.'

I resisted the schoolboy joke about the best way to get your own back.

———————

And back to the Sunday night party thrown for senators and House of Reps pollies by governor-general Sir Peter Cosgrove. I had a delightful and informative ten minutes alone with him before he excused himself by saying, 'Sorry, I'm being eyeballed.'

He told me how Yarralumla was meant to be a temporary home for the GG but, when the Depression hit, all thoughts of moving or rebuilding went out the window.

Weird, isn't it? Years after Federation (and after parliament moved from Melbourne's Exhibition Building to

Foggy Bottom) the Lodge was temporary. Parliament House was temporary. And now I learn Yarralumla was meant to be temporary.

I did learn a juicy vice-regal snippet. The GG told me he used to be an aide-de-camp at Government House back in 1972. And now the much-decorated soldier lives there as chief honcho.

Okay. AB bloody CC. 'Hinch the flip-flopper', 'Hinch the weathervane'. I, on the other hand, hope what I did during and after the long summer break actually showed some common sense.

In the final days of parliament last year, Nick X and I teamed up to push the government on some vital subcontractor amendments in the Building Code and ABCC, which passed and that I thought would make us the tradies' friends (through whistleblower protection, and invoice protection when a builder was going broke).

Not so. Over the break, I talked to subbies and mid-level and small developers. Their mood—especially regarding the negotiated two-year delayed starting date—can be summed up by the bloke in overalls in my local post office: 'What the [bleep] are you doing to us? I'll be broke in two years!'

Emailers complained that even nine months was too long.

I figured if I had voted to pass a law that would actually hurt the people we were supposedly trying to help, then I was wrong.

I called the PM and told him I'd accept the nine months.

The travel expenses scandal that forced the resignation of health minister Sussan Ley prompted a memory about how to pronounce people's names. 'Lay' or 'Lee'? A lot of newsreaders couldn't make up their minds. Like Deborah Kerr (Carr) or Graham Kerr (Care)?

Actress Janet Leigh (who, after *Psycho*, turned people off taking showers) pronounced her name 'Lay'. That prompted a piece of graffiti I saw on the wall of a Hollywood nightclub toilet: 'Janet lay is the best lee in town.'

'HINCH SELLS OUT WORKERS. SHAME.'

16 February 2017

Julia Gillard and Cory Bernardi both famously claimed that they took out their hatchets because each of their respective parties had 'lost its way'.

Might or might not be true, but I know of one senator who literally lost her way the other day. No names, no pack drill (oh, okay, it was Senator Jane Hume). Let me just say that I wouldn't advise you to let this Hume navigate you down a highway.

I was sitting in my office with my staff, going through the order of business for the day, when a woman appeared at the door. Not the front door. She had come through the reception area, through the staff-desk area and through a fourth door, ending up about a foot from my desk.

An embarrassed Senator Hume went the colour of the Senate chamber as she realised her office was on the floor above us. Her map-lapse excuse: 'I haven't had my morning coffee yet.'

———————

Pot calling kettle black. The night before, I'd been guesting on *Paul Murray Live* and, as I left the Sky studio at 10 p.m., I took a 'short cut' towards the Senate exit and a shuttle ComCar.

'Tonnes of time ... the shuttle doesn't shut down until 10.30 p.m.,' I thought. I made it with just ten minutes to spare, after wandering lost in a deserted maze for twenty minutes.

———————

Speaking of corridors and the size of Parliament House, I almost missed a vital division this week, which would probably have warranted a censure motion or even a Hinch resignation.

The Senate bells rang for a key vote on the ABCC—a matter that was only before us again because of my change of position. The division bells were called unexpectedly, giving us four minutes to get to the chamber.

As the clock lights started flashing and the bells started ringing, I was five or six minutes away, in Bill Shorten's office. It was a mad corridor dash (while wearing that knee brace) and I just made it.

One Labor wit pointed out that the opposition leader missed an opportunity: he should have locked me in his office for a few minutes.

———————

And still on the ABCC controversy: in the Senate I described how I returned to Melbourne from Canberra to find a CFMEU tent outside my office with a banner saying, 'Hinch sells out workers. Shame.'

The union also started bombarding the Justice Party's and my personal Facebook pages with claims that I was in favour of robbing Australian workers of precious jobs by increasing 457 visas.

I said on Facebook:

This is such a despicable, lying, orchestrated CFMEU campaign. In the Building Code amendments last year, I voted with the Labor Party to make it compulsory for companies to advertise nationally for Australian workers (plus other conditions) before applying for 457 visas. Unlike Labor under industrial relations minister Shorten, who brought 457 imports in to work at KFC.

In the office-building lift that day, a man who had just seen the union protest shook my hand and said, 'You must be doing something right if you've made an enemy out of that mob.'

Who would have thought that Senator Mitch Fifield is a crooner? Even if he did return from the summer break with a beard and wearing R.M. Williams. Perhaps he was just cloning yours truly.

At a Senate function to celebrate commercial radio, the looming changes to the media-reach laws were the elephant in the room. The minister for communications said he didn't know Bill Shorten was such a Meat Loaf fan, when they discussed media reach and suddenly burst into a pretty good rendition of 'Two Out of Three Ain't Bad'.

Better than the old rasper's now notorious rendition at the grand final at the MCG.

Among the guests at the soiree in the members' dining room alcove were Macquarie Radio's Russell Tait and Adam Lang. I told Senator Fifield, 'If you ever have trouble with me in the Senate, blame him,' and pointed at Lang. 'He was the man who sacked me from 3AW. If he hadn't, then I wouldn't be here.'

Ben Fordham was the MC. He interviewed a couple of well-known blokes from the other side of the media: TV's David Speers and Kieran Gilbert.

Turns out they both got their start in regional radio, Gilbert in Cairns and Speers in Geelong. Speers jumped from K rock in Geelong to be an FM traffic reporter in Melbourne. Now he's a traffic cop with pollies who try to get lies past him.

Last Thursday was my seventy-third birthday. A journo asked me if I even imagined on my seventy-second birthday that I'd be spending this one in the Senate.

I told him that anything was possible. 'I spent my seventieth birthday in jail, and the first birthday greeting that day was a gruff "Happy birthday, Hinch" from a guard at the 6 a.m. line-up.'

SCANDAL, RUMOURS AND SCURRILOUS ACCUSATIONS

23 February 2017

I well remember a farcical Neil Simon play called *Rumors*. Wasn't his best, but it stuck in my memory, probably more than in most people's, because the Australian production, at Melbourne's Comedy Theatre, starred my then-wife Jacki Weaver and former fiancée Lynda Stoner.

I imagine they could have started some rumours of their own.

Somebody should write a political version of the play and base it in Canberra. The place thrives on rumours, survives on rumours.

I harvested a few this week, even though neither the Senate nor 'the other place' was sitting. The most serious rumour actually came from inside *Crikey!* The email said:

> I have heard from a very reliable source that Senator Hinch has a doc naming a former [party leader], a former premier and several actors in a child trafficking ring.
>
> As a journo, I thought I should at least ask the rude question: Do you? And if you do what do you plan to do with it?
>
> Of course, I understand if you don't want to tell me, but I figured it could not hurt to ask.

My response: 'Wish I did. There has been an unverified letter floating around for several years naming everybody from [deleted] to [deleted]. I guess that's the one they're referring to. DH.'

I think it can be traced back to the Sydney days of gay activist lawyer John Marsden, who successfully sued Channel Seven for defamation around the time of unsubstantiated (if credible) allegations regarding rent boys around the El Alamein Fountain in Kings Cross.

The problem, then and now, is that whenever I have got close to publication, no source would agree to be identified and step into the witness box in my defence when the inevitable defamation writs hit me. No proof. No story.

One rumour I hope is true: with the government's new-found love for 'clean' coal, and ScoMo taking a chunk of it into 'the other place' as an accessory, there is scuttlebutt that environment minister Josh Frydenberg is looking for some way to keep Hazelwood open. That would save 800 jobs.

Problem is, the pollution-belching plant was built (in environmentally ignorant days), with a life expectancy of fifty years. And that deadline ran out in the late 1990s.

Late last year, in the final days of sittings, the House of Reps speaker and the Senate president pushed through measures to build an expensive new security fence across the majestic Parliament House lawns.

The house passed it unanimously. Only the Greens and *moi* spoke against it in the Senate. I said it was like 'putting barbed wire on the Opera House'. I have since learned from Senate president Stephen Parry that the contract has gone out. So sad.

At the time, an *Age* journalist called me to follow up on a rumour that there was a plan to build a moat around the joint. I laughed. I have since found out it was true. Prime minister Tony Abbott had to be talked out of it.

Bit like President Nixon when he wanted new uniforms to make White House guards look like they were from Ruritania.

———————

Another rumour, closer to home, which one journo passed along, was sort of my own doing: had Hinch been seen 'falling down drunk'?

I actually predicted the rumour. One night, my staff waited back while I gave an adjournment speech about Victoria needing a new numberplate. Not 'Victoria: The Garden State' or 'Victoria: The Place To Be' but 'Victoria: The Crime State'. (We put the video up on the Justice Party Facebook page, to reach more than 500 000 people. It was viewed by more than 200 000. Are you listening, Premier Dan Andrews?)

Afterwards we repaired, as they say, to the Ostani Restaurant at the Hotel Realm, for a late pizza. They have the best, freshest-tasting pizza dough in Canberra.

The place has one drawback: lots of low, deceptive, badly lit steps. Ten minutes after warning a newcomer of the hazard, I stepped out to take a phone call and made a spectacular pratfall.

My immediate reaction was not that I'd hurt my knee-braced leg. It was 'Great, now somebody will say "Hinch is back on the sauce".'

Ah, Canberra. Ah, rumours. It's the capital's currency.

NEVER UNDER-ESTIMATE THE ESTIMATES

2 March 2017

'Beware the Ides of March' was the Shakespearean warning. In Canberra, at this time of year, it's more a case of beware the Senate estimates committee hearings.

Talk about 'expect the unexpected'—as we used to say on the old *Hinch* current affairs program. Anything can come up when ministers, their department secretaries and public service honchos trudge up the Hill to umpteen public hearing rooms.

For a crossbencher, it's a triathlon, trying to juggle five or six committees a day (from 9 a.m. and up to 11 p.m.), and trying to anticipate when a Kim Carr or an Ian Macdonald will run out of filibustering puff, so you can get a turn.

The Legal and Constitutional Affairs Committee is always a gold-star event with the curmudgeonly aforementioned Macdonald in the chair. Recently, he abruptly adjourned the hearing for several 'cooling off' periods as the government members tried to delay the heralded interrogation of attorney-general George Brandis over allegations he misled the Senate last November about the WA/Bond/Bell/ATO/$300 million scandal about whether he instructed the AG counsel not to argue a particular way in the High Court.

When the questions finally came (mainly from senators Watt, Wong and Hinch), Brandis adopted the Arthur Sinodinos 'I don't recall' defence. On that one, the fat lady has not yet sung.

I said 'expect the unexpected', and that's why I was quoting Weary Dunlop and Gough Whitlam at the Foreign Affairs and Defence Department Committee hearing.

At a time when our veterans are killing themselves at an alarming rate and post-traumatic stress disorder is rampant, it is worth remembering that Weary once said, 'Get men working at arts and crafts in the hospital thereby helping them acquire an interest in life.'

And Gough? Well, the former prime minister, as Flight Lieutenant EG Whitlam, was the last military-veteran PM. And he once said, 'Of all the objectives of my government, none had a higher priority than the encouragement of the arts, the preservation and enrichment of our cultural and intellectual heritage.'

The estimates connection? I recently discovered a Diggers' group called the Australian National Veterans Arts Museum. For about three years, they have been trying to acquire a Defence Department building on St Kilda Road in Melbourne. It's an amazing Art Deco building that is part of the Queen Victoria Barracks' 'footprint' and just across from The Shrine. It is heritage listed.

It was built in 1937 as a vital rehab centre for World War I veterans and has been vacant for twenty years. Yep, twenty years.

The vets have been in talks with Victorian premier Dan Andrews, Melbourne lord mayor Robert Doyle, and Brendan Nelson from the Australian War Memorial. Promisingly, Labor made its acquisition a federal election promise last year and pledged $10 million.

Guess what? The government has decided 'it is no longer needed' and put it up for commercial sale. The department wants it sold in the next ten months. The sale has to be stopped.

An estimates scandal, courtesy of BuzzFeed journalist/blogger Alice Workman. She was watching the much-anticipated appearance of the $5 million postie, Ahmed Fahour, and tweeted: *After all of One Nation's criticism of the Australia Post CEO's $5.6 million salary, no one from PHON is in the room #estimates.* And she posted a pic to prove it.

It prompted this response from Senator Malcolm Roberts, apparently stung by the pictorial empirical evidence: *As much as we would have loved to be there to grill Board on #auspost salaries, Australians have us working on more important issues today.*

One Nation's organ grinder, and Pauline Hanson's chief adviser, James Ashby, obviously had other ideas. The 'more important issues' were put on hold, and Roberts popped up in a committee room several hours later.

His NSW colleague Senator Brian Burston, looking decidedly out of sorts, was also spotted in Aussie's Cafe after a quick flight from Sydney. No Pauline, though.

Hoisted by his own petard.

I poked fun at Liberal senator Jane Hume, who got confused and wandered absent-mindedly into my Senate office. Hers is a floor above.

I wrote: 'No names, no pack drill (oh, okay, it was Senator Jane Hume). Let me just say that I wouldn't advise you to let this Hume navigate you down a highway.' After one late-night estimates session, I met a fresh-faced young bloke named Luke. In my office.

We shook hands and, just as I was about to ask what he was doing there, it dawned on me: I'd walked out of the lift into the wrong office. Senator Hume's office. One floor above mine.

Welcome to estimates week.

THE TRICK: JUST TALK, LECTURE, HECTOR

9 March 2017

As a newbie in the Senate, I'm the first to point out that I am not totally au fait with procedural matters and terms like 'Point of order, Mr President'.

And never is that more obvious than at estimates committee hearings when some government committee chairmen/women find it hard to conceal their disdain (at times sheer loathing) for Labor and Greens senators. And try to gag them.

The same can be said for government ministers when forced to sit for hours as witnesses—for their own portfolios or the ministers they represent from 'the other place'— facing a horseshoe of inquisitors who can't be shut down by the usual digital clock on the Senate chamber wall.

One of the tactics is the filibuster, so that embarrassing issues can get jammed for time. The other one is to give the longest answers possible and therefore eat up an inquisitor's assigned fifteen minutes—time doled out at the chair's discretion.

The trick is to just talk and talk, lecture, hector, be pedantic. Anybody think I'm talking about attorney-general George Brandis here?

He's so good at it that, at one recent hearing, with Brandis at the witness table, I called a point of order in the middle of my own questions. I asked the chair if such verbose answers were coming out of my precious fifteen minutes.

Some pollies are so good at it they can even talk on the inhale—so you can't even force an interjected follow-up question while they are taking a breath. Malcolm Fraser was a master at that technique on radio, I reckon there was one interview with Big Mal where he only answered about five questions in thirty minutes.

That's why some of our esteemed leaders insist on only appearing live on TV with journalists Ray Martin or Hinch or David Speers or Laurie Oakes. Nothing to do with fearing their answers could be doctored or taken out of context. It's that they know they can jawbone you to death and hit a commercial break before the killer question can be fired.

That's also why a question like Richard Carleton's 'blood on your hands' opener to Bob Hawke, after he rolled Bill Hayden, was such a zinger. Everybody knew it was on from the get-go.

***

Recently, I've found myself saying, 'I know I sound like a politician' when I know I'm sounding like a politician. It's when I'm asked, repeatedly, and understandably, how I am enjoying this career swerve so late in life.

The answer I give is: 'It's much harder work than I thought. There's so much paperwork. You've got to be across everything.' And that's not just the issues you and your party campaigned on.

This will sound self-serving, but the paper flood is even harder for a crossbencher than for a Liberal or Labor senator. When the bells ring for a division, they just have to follow the whip. That even applies, to a slightly lesser degree, to the Greens, the Nick Xenophon Team and One Nation. Follow the leader.

I was sitting in the chamber chatting with One Nation's Brian Burston when Pauline Hanson loomed and imperiously indicated he was sitting on the wrong side of the room for the vote.

I think Burston was mischievously playing silly buggers, because he waited until the bells stopped ringing and the clerks were closing the doors before ambling across the chamber to join Hanson and Malcolm Roberts.

———————

I'm beginning to think I must be a magnet for, shall we say, unusual ComCar drivers.

After one late-night estimates hearing last week, I headed out of the Senate portal to be asked the common question 'Front or back?' when the white shuttle car with the red-and-white plates pulled up.

Laden down with a bulging briefcase and a couple of bulky red files, and wanting to make some phone calls on the way back to the hotel, I indicated the back.

It prompted this exchange:

'You always sit in the back?'

'No—sometimes I sit in the front, but I've got some work to do.'

Stony silence. Then 'I thought only royalty sat in the back.'

Maybe it was because I'd just spent fifteen hours straight in the word factory. Maybe it was because I've always thought it a wank when pollies, wearing $1000–$2000 suits, thought it made them 'men of the people' to sit in the front seat. Maybe it was because when I hire a taxi or a limo, at my expense,

I sit in the back. Maybe I was just tired, but I said: 'Only royalty? Well, Nikita Khrushchev always sat in the back in those crappy black cars in communist Moscow.'

The rest of the trip was conducted in silence.

THEY DONE HIM PROUD

16 March 2017

It was a foetid August day in New York in 1973. It was before pooper-scoopers, so the hot summer pavements in Manhattan reeked of dog shit. Even on Fifth Avenue. (By the end of August, you believed Johnny Carson was right when he claimed on TV that New Jersey folk would sneak across the Hudson River at night to let their dogs dump in New York.)

For me, that steamy August day was even shittier than usual. I was at the run-down, paint-peeling-off-the-walls New York City morgue to identify the body of my friend and colleague Lillian Roxon.

The extreme heat had brought on a fatal asthma-induced heart attack, and the Fairfax foreign correspondent and author of *Lillian Roxon's Rock Encyclopaedia* was suddenly dead at forty-one.

I identified her body and then trudged back to work to write her obituary. That's what journos did, and do. No human resources officer. No counselling. Time for that in the pub, over umpteen drinks, but not until after you'd filed your story. Don't be a sook.

That image of dear Lillian, on a slab under a grubby grey blanket, flooded back to me when the *Oz* tweeted that Bill Leak was dead.

So unexpected. So tragic. So soon. And I thought of his mates, gutted, but still geared to getting a paper out. Do it for Bill. Grieve later.

His colleagues, as my gran would say, 'done him proud'.

I'll stay with my initial Twitter reaction: *Oh, no. Cannot be.*

I was in Brisbane for a public hearing of the Senate Legal and Constitutional Affairs Committee, of which I am an avid participating member.

Nauru, Manus and refugees were again the issues under investigation/interrogation.

The Turnbull/Obama/Trump 'people swap' deal is inching to a denouement.

Hinch's Hunch (and it is purely that) is that the initial agreement with former president Barack Obama was for about 1200 detainees to be accepted into the US and we would take a similar number of South Americans currently held in Costa Rica.

The Trump demand for 'extreme vetting' will cause that number to come down to about 900. The anti-refugee prez can claim his vigilance paid off. Would-be terrorists and Boston bombers weeded out. The PM can say the deal was honoured. Win-win.

I have supported the government/Labor policy of offshore processing. But. There is no legit reason why we have not had a child commissioner on Nauru, because there are still forty-five children there.

I do not support a lifetime ban on people sent back to their country of origin or resettled elsewhere. That is cruel and unjust.

It is also a disgrace that some women, who were allegedly sexually assaulted on Nauru and were brought here to the mainland for treatment, must 'return to the scene of the crime' if they want to be considered for resettlement in the United States. That is inhumane.

You've got to hand it to Mathias Cormann. He really is an Antipodean Schwarzenegger. It's not just the accent. He is a verbal brick wall. Just look at him on *Insiders* on Sunday. The Libs and WA premier Colin Barnett had just been flushed down the *scheissen hausen*, partly because of the preference deal with One Nation that Cormann had so cleverly negotiated.

Barrie Cassidy couldn't lay a glove. The interview must have gone twelve minutes and we learned nothing, except that 'contrition', 'whoops', 'my mistake' and 'we were wrong' are obviously not part of the WA Libs' lexicon.

And on that misguided, desperate, ill-fated preference deal with Pauline Hanson, talk about the perils of getting too close to Pauline. It obviously did hurt both parties, but don't forget her personal performance, in that final, giddy week on the ground, during which One Nation's numbers plummeted.

Calling Vladimir Putin a hero, getting into bed with the anti-vaxxers and being caught telling lies about her support for siphoning some of Queensland's GST to WA was all her own klutzy work.

RISKY RIDE ON THE OMNIBUS

23 March 2017

In a typical burst of frankness, Jacki Weaver once confessed that, when she was a struggling young actress in Sydney—decades before becoming a Hollywood doyenne—she stole a bottle of milk from a neighbour's verandah.

She was a single mum with a young son. She'd haul him along to auditions, and often babysitting duties would be performed by musicians in the orchestra pit.

There was no such thing as a single mothers' pension or childcare benefits.

How things change. I thought of that when confronted by the massive omnibus bill this week and, I'll admit, I helped give the vehicle a couple of flat tyres. (It's called an 'omnibus bill' because it's a heap of controversial individual bills in one big vehicle package—which the government hopes it can drive through the Senate.)

Don't get me wrong. I supported most of the changes to the childcare subsidies—especially the lowest-wage earners, including many single mums, getting 86 per cent of their childcare subsidised.

But (not having any young children) I was shocked, absolutely stunned, by an impressive government graph that showed wealthy Australian families, earning between \$350 000 and \$500 000 a year, had been getting a 50 per cent rebate on childcare. That is Noddyland.

It is true the omnibus bill tapered those benefits after \$250 000 but it still gave some taxpayer rebate dollars to people earning half a million a year.

This was one cross crossbencher. I held out and the government finally agreed to support my amendment cutting childcare subsidies to zero for households earning \$350 000.

I would have liked the kick-in level to be lower but I'm learning that 75 per cent of something is better than 100 per cent of nothing.

———————

I'm glad *Insiders* picked up on a rather telling vignette from Bill Leak's memorial at the Sydney Town Hall last Friday.

Tony Abbott was one of the last to arrive. He had that jaw-clenched, cycling-into-the-wind look as he searched for his seat in the front row where Malcolm and Lucy Turnbull, John Howard and Barry Humphries were already sitting. Studiously avoiding eye contact with the Turnbulls, he shook Bazza's hand, couldn't find his seat and then realised he had to double back.

On the return run he again avoided the PM and lunged for the hand of the editor-in-chief of the *Oz*, Paul Whittaker.

I can sympathise a bit. For the AFL grand final breakfast one year, I had my invite but no place card at the huge head table. After a couple of embarrassing trips up and back, in front of 1000 people, I spotted Ron Barassi's tag, so grabbed his seat. I figured he was so famous they'd find him a spot. Never admitted that before. Sorry, Barass.

———————

After a gosh–golly tour of Sky's new whiz-bang CNN/Fox/London Sky-style studio in Sydney—and a fascinating first-time appearance with a new TV media star Adam Giles on *PM Live*—I bumped into One Nation senator Malcolm Roberts.

He was there for the second hour of the Paul Murray talkfest—which, actually, is rating better at times than the first hour. Both are much better raters than Andrew Bolt, who doesn't even hit 30 000 to make the Foxtel top twenty and is beaten by upstarts Peta Credlin and Kristina Keneally. But that's another media story.

I had just been surprised, on air, by a clip of Pauline Hanson, alongside tireless justice crusader Bruce Morcombe, announcing her support for a national public register of convicted sex offenders. I was tempted to say, 'What took you so long?' but, on this issue, I'll take (because I need it) all the support I can get, and I was gracious about it. I just wish the government or the Labor opposition would embrace it.

(To be fair, I have had the PM pull out his mobile phone and activate an American app to find a convicted sex offender whose details—name, photo, address, crimes, sentence—are required to be registered under Megan's Law, which has been in effect federally in the US since 1996.)

When I mentioned the sex offenders register and his leader to Senator Roberts, he looked at me strangely. 'Aghast' wouldn't be an exaggeration.

'Oh, I thought you meant Pauline was on the sex offenders register.'

Wouldn't be dead for quids, as my father would say. When he was really enjoying himself in some mundane fashion, Dad would smile and say, 'I wonder what the rich people are doing?'

––––––––

In a 50-plus-year career in newspapers, radio and television, I filled a few executive positions and, when a staffer left, the cry would go up at their farewell drinks, 'C'mon, Hinchey, give us the train speech.'

Here it is: 'If a train pulls into a station and you don't get on it and it goes to somewhere you discover you'd have liked to have gone—then it's your own fucking fault.'

THE PENALTY OF PENALTY RATES

30 March 2017

My brother Des is visiting Canberra from across the ditch, and he reminded me of the day when, as a 10-year-old kid, he went to the shop to get a tin of golden syrup.

He went to put it on the account, and the shopkeeper refused. He told my brother: 'No. Your parents have no money.' And he trudged home, empty-handed. That was back when, four years younger than him, I wore his hand-me-down short trousers.

I thought of that time after I said I would abide by the umpire's decision and accept the Fair Work Commission call for a cut in Sunday penalty rates. And the email and Twitter insults poured in: *What would you fuckers with your snouts in the trough know about doing it tough? What would you silver spoons and nobs know about the workers? What would you know about being broke?* Et cetera, et cetera, et cetera, as Yul Brynner would say.

My personal adult nadir was the day I stood at the ATM in the Victorian country town of Woodend on a Saturday morning and saw my balance was $6.49. The minimum withdrawal was twenty dollars, so I had no money at all. Which is why, for a year, I lived on two-minute noodles, in my Grizzly Adams period. And then I went to do radio on 5DN in Adelaide and my climb back up the financial mountain began.

———

But back to Sunday penalty rates. My position on them has been very public since my radio days. I have said they should be the same as Saturday rates. And I know a lot of small business owners agree.

But, in my maiden speech, I promised that I would listen to people. I said I supported the umpire's position. I still do— but I decided to go to the third umpire. That's the review umpire: the Sunday workers, the single mothers, the university students who study all week and only work on Sundays. I listened.

On my senator's salary, a few bucks, more or less, doesn't mean much. But, as outlined above, I remember the days when it did.

As a party leader, I have to remember that the argument should not be about my personal circumstances or personal opinion. It has to be about what's best for the community.

That's why I told the Senate, 'I've consulted the third umpire and the third umpire's decision is that cuts to Sunday penalty rates are O-U-T, OUT.'

———————

I gained some valuable experience in the Senate the other night as the government shrewdly cut their omnibus in half and negotiated both halves of the bus through the upper house minefield.

It was a bruising, but valuable, political lesson as we rode the omnibus bill to its nocturnal destination.

Finance minister Mathias Cormann was negotiating with me and Senator David Leyonhjelm over our amendments to cut off any government subsidies for wealthy families.

At the risk of having my Melbourne office blocked by Toorak tractors (SUVs) I moved that the subsidy go to zero from incomes of $350 000. Leyonhjelm wanted to go further: for childcare subsidies to start tapering off from $200 000 and end at $350 000.

We both agreed to vote for each other's amendments and then vote for the government bill. I put that to Cormann and—needing our votes for an extension to sitting hours—the finance minister agreed.

The LDP senator's amendment failed, mine passed. The bill passed and Leyonhjelm tweeted: *I & @humanheadline stopped childcare subsidies for $350K incomes, but reduction for $200–$350 K blocked by Labor, Greens & Coalition.*

Senator Leyonhjelm omitted to say that, while he supported my amendment to stop childcare subsidies after $350 000, he did not then vote for the bill. At the last minute, he told me he was abstaining because 'I have to think of my constituents.' While the bells were ringing for four minutes, he turned to flee the chamber. I thought that if I was going to be ratted on, it would be in public, and managed to keep him engaged in conversation until the Senate president called, 'Lock the doors,' and there was no escape.

Senator Leyonhjelm then sat on the abstention bench along with Senator Cory Bernardi, who told me, 'I didn't make an agreement with anybody.'

As he came down off the bench, Leyonhjelm boasted, 'I got away with it.'

I said, 'Not with me you didn't.'

Lesson learned.

LUNCH WITH JOHN HOWARD

6 April 2017

The CFMEU was on the six o'clock news (again) recently when they hooted and hollered and tried to intimidate former prime minister John Howard as he took a lunchtime stroll near Sydney's Martin Place.

A pity the union protesters hadn't waited and been there a few weeks later. They could have figuratively (or maybe not) killed two birds with one stone: him and me.

I was in Sydney to have lunch with Howard, at my request, and we did get some soap-opera-style double takes as we walked together to a city restaurant.

Over the decades, our relationship had been fairly antagonistic. The TV and radio heavy grilling the treasurer/opposition leader/prime minister. I asked him to break bread with me because I was impressed with his new career as a TV presenter in the series he did for the ABC on Bob Menzies. Frankly, I was surprised to find myself enjoying his interviews with Clive James and Bob Hawke and Thomas Keneally.

As we sat down, I observed: 'The politician turned media star lunches with the media star turned politician. Who would have thunk it?' What odds of that reversal even a couple of years ago?

The Rod Culleton and Bob Day electoral imbroglios (both men have now lost their Senate seats) send some obvious messages to all politicians but a special one to crossbench senators. A cogent one is that all minor parties must, in future, stand a minimum of three candidates in any Senate race.

Day resigned from the Senate when his building company went into liquidation but the High Court also found he was ineligible for the 2016 poll because, under section 44, he had an inappropriate pecuniary interest in a contract with the Commonwealth about an electoral office lease. In Culleton's case, the High Court ruled he was ineligible to stand because, at the time of the election, he had been convicted of larceny—even though the charge was later annulled.

In Western Australia, One Nation stood three candidates: Culleton at No. 1, followed by his brother-in-law, Peter Georgiou, at No. 2 and Culleton's wife, Ioanna Culleton, at No. 3. Although Culleton was ruled ineligible, that still left two One Nation candidates in the race, which preserved PHON's vital above-the-line status and gave the seat to Georgiou.

In South Australia, Family First might not be so lucky. If the Culleton situation applied, a recount—supervised by a single High Court judge—would elect the other Family First candidate, Lucy Gichuhi. But with Day out of the picture, Family First really had only one candidate on election day. That was not enough to form a party ticket for above-the-line voting.

(There are now belated questions about Kenyan-born Gichuhi's possible dual citizenship, which would rule her out too under section 44. And that could reignite the debate about Tony Abbott's citizenship.)

Labor, with an intense vested interest, has argued that all Family First's above-the-line votes should be discarded because the countback would probably then elect another Labor senator. That would give Labor twenty-seven Senate votes and twenty-eight if (as the Libs do) you include Jacqui Lambie.

The High Court ruling seemed to go in favour of Family First getting the nod. The judgment said that if those votes were disregarded, it would 'constitute a most serious distortion of the real intention of many thousands of voters', mainly those Family First-ers who voted above the line.

The government will be hoping that's the way the cookie crumbles.

On my Senate desk I have a miniature furphy, as a reminder of my visit to their Shepparton factory last year. The fifth-generation family company came to mind last week as the Senate sat past midnight and into an extra day as we battled over section 18c of the *Racial Discrimination Act* and then the cuts to company tax.

Labor opposed any cuts to company tax for turnovers of more than $2 million—even though Bill Shorten had lauded such cuts in the past. Some crossbenchers (me included) had greenlighted cuts for companies with turnovers up to $10 million.

That's where my little furphy ornament came in. I realised that this true-blue, Aussie-as-you-can-get family company, employing 150 Victorians, would not benefit from those cuts.

I said on the Senate floor, 'Lifting the threshold from 10 million to 50 million will mean that nearly 900 000 small-to-medium-sized companies, employing more than 4 million workers, will get tax cuts.'

I also thought of Gippsland, where closures are really making things tough for employers and employees alike. Places like Gippsland Aeronautics, which employs seventy-five people. They would have missed out on any cuts if we'd stuck to $10 million.

Interesting to see now if the government has wedged the opposition. Haven't yet seen Messrs Shorten and Leigh vow to repeal the cuts.

———

How's this for a double standard? Imagine if a couple of male senators started sniggering and making loud, unflattering remarks about a female senator who appeared to have spent too much time at the snack table during non-sitting weeks.

That's what recently happened in reverse, when Senator Sam Dastyari, testing the buttons on his white shirt, was called to the floor to scrutinise a division vote.

Two female senators called out things like 'What's that hanging over your belt, Dasher?' and 'You've porked up a bit, Sam.'

Pssst ... it's true. But, typically, Dasher's making self-deprecating jokes about it.

SAUSAGE ETIQUETTE ON THE CAMPAIGN TRAIL

13 April 2017

In my first editorial on my *Hinch Live* program on Sky News on Sunday nights, I invoked the wrath of right-wing commentator Gerard Henderson, and his dog, by questioning Tony Abbott's citizenship. And thereby his constitutional right under section 44 to even represent the good folk of Warringah, let alone be prime minister of this country. Had he renounced his British citizenship before first being elected in 1994?

The then-PM's office didn't help by sealing the records so the Aussie version of the 'birther movement' couldn't know if they were barking up the wrong family tree or not.

It all came up again when the Bob Day Senate shemozzle played out in the High Court. With the court ruling that Day, South Australia's No. 1 on the Family First Senate ticket, was ineligible, the spotlight then shone on their No. 2 candidate, Kenyan-born lawyer Lucy Gichuhi.

Gichuhi confirmed she had adopted Australian citizenship (but wouldn't say when) at an uncomfortable, stilted media conference but then clammed up when asked if she had renounced her Kenyan passport. In a later ABC radio interview, she said, 'I reserve the right to (not) discuss that topic any further.'

The Kenyan High Commission may have thrown her a life jacket by explaining that when Kenya's new constitution was promulgated in 2010, any person who took up the citizenship of another country ceased to be a Kenyan unless they reapplied for dual citizenship. And Lucy Gichuhi had not.

That may not be the only obstacle in the way of her taking Bob Day's seat. Family First stood only two candidates in the 2 July 2016 election. Labor will argue, with merit, that, with only one candidate left in the race, Family First can no longer be regarded as a group so as to attract above-the-line votes.

Even if Gichuhi gets Day's below-the-line votes, that would not be enough to beat another would-be Labor senator. Stay tuned.

At the risk of upsetting Gerard (and his dog) again, it is worth going back to the eligibility of Tony Abbott. Why won't he release proof of his British citizenship renunciation?

A couple of years ago, about 40000 people signed a petition demanding he do just that.

Back then, I said on Sky, 'I run a real risk of being labelled a nutter here.' I was well aware of the birther movement in the United States, with people, especially Donald Trump, claiming for years that Barack Obama's presidency was illegal. They claimed he was really born in Kenya. Not Hawaii. And if you're not born in the United States, you can't be president. Some cranks still believe the Kenyan-birth conspiracy, even though the White House produced Obama's Hawaiian birth certificate.

Who would have thunk it? That thirty-three years after this interview with PM Malcolm Fraser, the bearded bloke on the left would be a senator.

On the campaign trail in Melbourne.

Campaigning for medicinal cannabis at Nimbin MardiGrass. The very pregnant woman was not a user.

Just after I received the ceremonial gold pass from the Usher of the Black Rod.

Signing the official book after swearing in. With Liberal senator Jane Hume. *David Foote/Auspic/DPS*

Executive Assistant Annette Philpott in our makeshift office during the first week.

Sharing a joke with opposition senate leader Penny Wong.
Mike Bowers/The Guardian

A lighter moment in PM Malcolm Turnbull's office under THE Olsen.

My escort to the Mid-Winter Ball. Sadly, Jacqui Lambie resigned over her dual citizenship. *Mike Bowers/The Guardian*

Being subjected to the hard word by Nick Xenophon. I'll miss him. *David Foote*

The moment my motion to end restrictions on senate photographers was passed on the voices. *Mike Bowers/The Guardian*

Finger painting with a young Syrian refugee on a Save the Children visit to Lebanon.

In one refugee camp in Jordan, 80 000 people live in conditions like this.

A rainbow warrior. Showing off my marriage equality scarf to attorney-general George Brandis. *Alex Ellinghausen*

King of the stunts. Sam Dastyari surprised me with a
wedding cake—and a kiss. *AAP*

Something a lot of others wished they'd had.
Proof I was not a dual citizen when elected.

It's different here. You can be born overseas but must be an Australian citizen to hold office and you can't hold two passports. No dual citizenship. You must renounce the country of your birth. Section 44 of the constitution says you must not hold the citizenship of any 'foreign power'.

Anthony John Abbott was born in England in 1957. The family emigrated to Australia in 1960. He became an Australian citizen in 1981, after winning a Rhodes Scholarship to Oxford as a Briton.

So, when did he renounce his British citizenship? We don't know.

The official line from the PM's office was: 'The Prime Minister is an Australian citizen and does not hold citizenship of any other country.'

Normally, you can check these things with the National Archives of Australia, which keeps all citizenship applications on public file. But, for some reason, the archives made Abbott's 1981 application confidential.

This all may sound far-fetched, but remember: Jackie Kelly had to stand again at a by-election after she was elected while holding Australian and New Zealand passports.

And some of you will remember Robert Wood. He was elected as a Nuclear Disarmament Party senator in 1987, and was thrown out in 1988 when it was discovered he was born in England and had not held an Australian passport prior to being elected.

As I said in the Senate last year, I believe all members of federal parliament should provide proof of eligibility to the speaker of the house or to the Senate president.

Better still: you should provide proof to the Australian Electoral Commission (AEC) the day you nominate.

How to get snagged by a snag.

During last year's marathon election campaign, we covered 11 250 kilometres through Victoria and NSW in the Justice Bus. That meant eating a lot of snags at the Country Fire Authority sausage sizzles—and too many magical meat pies from places like the Beechworth Bakery.

Even as an aspiring senator, I knew you don't turn down a proffered sausage smeared with tomato sauce on a slice of very ordinary bread. You'll get crucified by the media almost as much as they would attack you for eating it wrongly. Too daintily. Too phallicly.

Remember how the stand-up comics went after Donald Trump because of a campaign stop in Brooklyn where he was filmed eating a slice of pizza with a knife and fork? Something I do.

And so, Malcolm Turnbull got snagged when visiting flood-stricken Lismore. He turned down a sausage, ceremonially proffered by a Country Women's Association volunteer. Captured on the TV news, the PM delicately placed the sausage and paper plate back on the trestle table and said: 'That's lovely. That's very kind of you, but I think I am running around a bit much to be eating that.'

Reckon it was a coincidence that one Lycra-clad MAMIL, Tony Abbott, on his Pollie Pedal, later posted one particular tweet? It read, *Thank you Tumut Lions Club for manning the BBQ. Loved the snags and steak sandwiches!*

Yeah, a real man. Not like the Wentworth toff.

A GHASTLY STAIN OF COVER-UP

20 April 2017

The soon-to-be-concluded *Royal Commission into Institutional Responses to Child Sexual Abuse* is one of the most important inquiries this country has ever witnessed. Or, I hope, will ever witness.

What triggered it is a ghastly stain of cover-up in our churches and charities. But it remains, in my view, a jewel in Julia Gillard's troubled time in office.

Two points. I am fearful that, like so many past inquiries, any recommendations could be lost or buried, especially a vital national redress scheme. That is why I have lobbied for a joint parliamentary committee to be a watchdog, to make sure that whatever Justice Peter McClellan decrees is implemented.

It is why I have personal pledges from prime minister Malcolm Turnbull and opposition leader Bill Shorten to support such a committee, which they have agreed I shall chair. I will be introducing the matter at the next sitting of parliament in May.

But, having heaped that praise on the commission, I have also written to Justice McClellan requesting that he reopen his public hearings and correct what I believe is a serious flaw in them. We have seen interrogations of Catholics, Anglicans, the Salvation Army, Hillsong. What about Islamic schools and Muslim institutions?

Having a child bride is child rape. The mutilation of a girl's vagina is a sexual violation.

Going back to that issue of female genital mutilation (FGM). More than thirty years ago, I went to Africa to report on women being ostracised in their villages because they suffered from fistulas due to childbirth injuries and/or were victims of female genital mutilation.

I'm going to be crude here to explain why FGM is so putrid, so violent, so cruel, and is performed on innocent children.

Let me point something out: men were originally circumcised to prevent health problems. Girls are brutally circumcised to prevent later, adult, pleasure.

When young girls are circumcised in Africa, this is what happens. A child is held down, usually by her mother. A crone with a knife hacks off her clitoris. The child then has cow dung smeared on the wound to cause infection and form a scab. And her legs are tied together while that happens.

That's the stark truth.

The practice still goes on in Australia. As well as the Islamic and Hindu tradition of little girls being offered up as child brides.

FGM is illegal in Australia. So is raping a young girl as your 'bride'. Parents should be prosecuted. So should the person who performs the ceremony.

That's why I say the *Royal Commission into Institutional Responses to Child Sexual Abuse* has, sadly, dropped the ball by not investigating Islamic institutions. That's why I wrote to Justice McClellan.

———————

It was good to see the Turnbull–Dutton crackdown announcement on 457 visas—which let foreign workers into Australia to do specific jobs—even though there were predictably snide remarks about goat herders. It puzzled me how Bill Shorten had brazenly been making hay out of the issue when his confetti-like issuance of 457 visas while in office had led to McDonald's and KFC exploiting the system.

It shouldn't have surprised me. Nick Xenophon and I were savaged by the CFMEU and union Twitter trolls for 'giving Aussie jobs to 457 visas' when, in fact, last year we had forced Building Code and Australian Building and Construction Commission amendments that made it compulsory for Australian bosses to show cause and advertise nationally before a 457 could kick in.

I did succumb, though, and tweet: *Government crackdown on 457 visa rorts is good news. Justice Party not claiming credit.*

———————

Budget speculation is in full swing, and government ministers, as well as backbenchers, are running things up the flagpole to see who salutes. Super for first-home buyers. Pension breaks for downsizing seniors. First bad, second good.

It took me back to my childhood days with the walnut-veneer radiogram. We'd hear the hit parade top ten only once a week, on a Sunday night after the 'hospital request session' where people who were dying would hear 'You Will Never Grow Old'. Every week. And many of them wouldn't grow much older. Which wasn't the intended message.

What's the budget connection? On that same radiogram, my dad would play his favourite LP (as we called them), Billy Russell's *On Behalf of the Working Classes*.

The best line, and I remember it well: 'Promise them everything, give them nothing, and before you get it they take it off you.'

Sound familiar?

CREDIT WHERE CREDIT'S DUE

27 April 2017

I know it is officially called the opposition and, by name and by nature, that means an adversarial attitude, but, just occasionally, give us a break.

How about credit where credit is due? I'm sure the voters would appreciate it, because every single thing a government does cannot be wrong. Can't be bad for us.

I know, with recent governments of both persuasions, there are some cynics who would disagree with that premise.

But there was a classic case this week that, I believe, proves my point.

In recent months, a lot of people, inside and outside of Canberra, have been really worried by the Turnbull government's blinkered plan to slash millions of dollars from community legal centres and Legal Aid.

Many senators, including crossbenchers, thought it made a mockery of the government's so-called commitment to the campaign against domestic violence. It was obvious such cutbacks would add to the already scandalous delays in getting cases before the Family Court and would delay other wife-bashing cases in other courts.

There was genuine lobbying against it by the Law Council of Australia's Fiona McLeod, and I also talked to embattled reps from women's refuges. That was why I joined with Labor, the Greens and some other crossbenchers, to publicly oppose the cuts.

This week, attorney-general George Brandis announced that the CLC cuts planned for the budget had been cancelled.

I tweeted: *Federal Gov has dropped planned funding cuts for Community Legal Centres. We/you hollered. They listened. Great news.*

What did Labor do? Their professional sniper, Mark Dreyfus, himself a former attorney-general, and now shadow attorney-general, couldn't resist tweeting about the Brandis 'embarrassing backflip': *Reversal of CLC and ATSIL funding cuts today is very welcome, and a huge and embarrassing backflip for Brandis. #fundequaljustice.*

As I said, people and politicians hollered and a government heard us.

Talk about damned if you do ...

How about the poor voters in South Australia? Last year heaps of them voted for a devout and devoted candidate at the top of the Liberal Party ticket and, after a long, cushy junket at the United Nations, their man decamped—as Cory Bernardi announced his new Australian Conservatives party.

Others voted for Family First and narrowly re-elected Senator Bob Day. The High Court gave him the flick but then gave the nod to Family First's second choice, Lucy Gichuhi.

As of this week (what time is it?) Gichuhi is about to be sworn in as a senator but not a Family First senator. Her party has folded into Bernardi's right-wing rump, but she hasn't been convinced to join and will sit, at least for now, as an independent.

So, let's get this straight. Bernardi was elected as a Liberal. He's now not. Gichuhi was elected (appointed?) as a Family First senator. She's now not.

Two days after Anzac Day 2017, let me pass on a yarn from my dear departed dad, who served in the Solomon Islands in World War II.

After the landing at Guadalcanal, the Aussies and Kiwis saw a banner erected by US Marines. It boasted, 'We Won!!'

A laconic Digger added two words: 'We Helped!'

Lest We Forget.

'FREE THE WEED!'

4 May 2017

Who would have thunk it? A few years ago, who would have thought that backwater New Zealand, and religiously rigid Ireland, would allow same-sex couples to marry before Australia did?

Who would have thought that several states in the US would be legally selling recreational marijuana commercially before it was permitted here?

On that one, I was decades out. Back in 1969, as a foreign correspondent in New York, I was asked by Fairfax to write one of those prediction pieces about 'What will Australia look like at the end of the '70s?'

Hinch's Hunch was that by 1980 pot would be legalised in Australia. It wasn't wishful thinking. I was living in the 'anything goes—let it all hang out' Swinging Sixties. I'd written stories about Flower Power. Been to Haight-Ashbury. But I didn't smoke pot. Never did. Never will. Didn't even try the cookies. Booze was my drug of choice—and it was legal.

I'm going down that track because this weekend I'll be at Australia's pot paradise: the MardiGrass in Nimbin.

Last year, as a novice senatorial candidate, I went there to support the campaign for medical marijuana—legalising cannabis oil. One of my last stories for *Sunday Night* was about the miraculous effects cannabis oil was having on long-suffering spasming children. And why parents were risking jail to provide it.

That was why I was there, taking part in a bong-throwing competition (I came last), shouting 'Free the weed!', and leading the parade with a bare-bellied pregnant woman who displayed a marijuana leaf on her tummy.

And for those people who were shocked that a mother-to-be, who looked like the baby was dropping that afternoon, was a pothead: the pregnant woman was not a user. She was there with her husband and two other children because 'If usually conservative people like me don't get out and protest about legalising medical cannabis, the politicians will never listen and nothing will happen.'

That's why I'll be back there at the weekend.

––––––––––

On a light weekend across the ditch, I did some heavy reading—Chrissie Foster's harrowing book *Hell on the Way to Heaven*. This is the ghastly story of what happened to her family after two of her young daughters were molested by the evil Father Kevin O'Donnell at a Catholic girls' primary school.

Last week, I spent time with Chrissie and her indefatigably resolute husband, Anthony, as we dissected the national redress plans and what will happen after the royal commission into institutional abuse brings down its final report at year's end.

I share the Fosters' concerns that the government will go soft on the recommendations—if their reaction to the delayed release of last year's interim report is any indication.

Only days after that Melbourne meeting in my office to discuss redress tactics, we were suddenly at a state funeral for Anthony Foster. He had hit his head in a fall and did not recover.

Apropos of nothing, maybe, a John F Kennedy story has floated to the front of my political memory bank because of the increasingly bizarre pronouncements coming out of the mouth of The Donald as he celebrates (?) his first 100 days in the White House.

I'm still trying to get my head around Trump's take on the American Civil War and his claim that President Andrew Jackson—whose portrait Trump has moved into the Oval Office—was really angry about the Civil War and how it could have been avoided.

Forget that Jackson died sixteen years before the first Confederate bullet was fired.

Anyway, the quote about Kennedy surfaced during the Nixon presidency, after stories started to surface about JFK's infidelities: 'At least what Kennedy did was with consenting American women. Nixon did it to a country.'

INSIDER TRADING ON BUDGET DAY?

11 May 2017

For me, the biggest budget story was the banks. Not that they were going to be hit with a levy (aka a super tax) but that, despite the so-called lockup, the bash-the-banks news leaked at around 10 a.m. and $14 billion was wiped off the major bank stocks.

I have written to the AFP demanding a police investigation. Let's find out who the short-sellers were and did they have connections on the Hill?

––––––––––

The lockup of financial journalists is meant to be watertight (leakproof?), with no mobile phones, with escorts to the toilet, etc. It has become a joke, with the leaks—or government drops, to be more accurate. This year it almost caused a parliamentary crisis.

At a crossbench budget procedure briefing by the leader of the government in the Senate, George Brandis, and Senator Mitch Fifield, the issue about senators going into the lockup was raised. Could they leave if the division bells rang?

I raised it because the 45th parliament had had 198 divisions and I was the only senator with a perfect 198 voting record.

The attorney-general agreed that if anybody attempted to stop me performing my voting duties as an elected senator, that would be contempt of parliament.

Hence, I was a tad surprised on budget morning to receive an email from an A-G adviser warning me:

Consistent with standard practice in previous years, participants may enter the lock-up after 1.30pm but, once they have done so, cannot leave until 7.30pm, with the exception of Senators, who may leave the lock-up at 7.00pm. This means that Senators may NOT leave the lock-up for divisions.

I wrote back that I would be leaving if a division were called, and if security tried to impede me I would physically resist and have them charged with contempt of parliament.

Then I echoed that pledge on Neil Mitchell's 3AW program. Within an hour, the treasurer's department advised us that if a division were called, crossbenchers would be escorted as a group to the chamber. We could not talk to staff and surrendered phones must stay that way.

Luckily, the bells did not ring.

———————

At that same Brandis–Fifield briefing, the attorney-general was explaining how the Senate budget speeches Thursday night would be restricted to crossbench party leaders' and independents' replies.

He told One Nation's leader, Pauline Hanson, that meant she could speak but PHON's other three senators could not.

I interjected, 'Unless they become independents by Thursday.'

No hint of a smile from The Hanson or her shadow, James Ashby.

Especially when their own Senator Brian Burston mischievously cut in, 'I was just going to say that.'

———————

This was my first budget on the other side of the fence. It brought back some budget-night media memories. The 2017 newbies couldn't believe that the best budget-night parties were thrown by treasurer John Howard. They couldn't believe he would have a few drinks and hit the dance floor. They also couldn't believe that parliamentary staff used to sell booze to journos in the lockup.

———————

My favourite memory of a Treasurer Keating budget-night party was of being approached by Prime Minister Hawke. Cigar in hand, he was in a good mood.

It was around the time of renewed French underground nuclear tests at Mururoa atoll.

I asked the Silver Bodgie about Australia's reaction. The famous Hawke snarl came out: 'I don't like the fucking French either.' I had my story for the morning and it had nothing to do with the budget.

Some French official was visiting Australia at the time, and next day I saw him on TV being peppered with questions at a press conference in Brisbane.

———————

I hoped it was not an omen. The hundreds of copies of Scott Morrison's budget 2017–18 speech were all printed with the cover upside down.

———————

SENATOR HANSON: PLEASE EXPLAIN

18 May 2017

Senator Pauline Hanson didn't appear on *Sunrise* on Monday for our weekly Channel Seven breakfast-TV stoush. She was replaced by Senator Jacqui Lambie. No disrespect to Lambie, but I was disappointed.

I had a doozy of a 'please explain' for Senator Hanson, which had prompted this tweet: *Betrayal. Pauline Hanson trying to spin way out of No vote to cut red tape for medicinal cannabis. They betrayed sick kids and terminally ill.*

The political background to it was a Senate vote on a disallowance motion put by Greens leader Senator Richard Di Natale, which, if passed, would have cut red tape to make the importation of medical cannabis easier and so make it more available to desperate parents and cancer patients.

The division was tied 32–32 and a tie means the no vote wins. Senate law. President Stephen Parry does not have a casting vote, unlike Mr Speaker in 'the other place'.

In the lead-up to the vote, Di Natale was on a roller-coaster ride. At the last minute, Labor decided to support the Greens. I think (and who's a cynic?) they did the eleventh-hour jump because they had done their sums and knew it would fail.

The person who hadn't done his sums was Di Natale. He assumed (definition: an ass out of you and me) that One Nation would cast their four votes in his favour. After all, in the July election Pauline Hanson's face had beamed out of posters extolling the virtues of medicinal marijuana.

I was sitting next to Di Natale and saw the look of disbelief when a redhead appeared in the 'no' seats. The Xenophon team of three also voted no.

It really saddened me because that Senate vote physically hurt vulnerable, suffering Australians, young and old. Spasming babies and terminally ill adult cancer patients.

To make it worse, I was at MardiGrass in Nimbin the weekend before, talking to parents of little kids who have had 900 epileptic spasms that were made smoother by the use of medicinal cannabis oil. I took part in a medical cannabis debate up there. I met a man who spent ten months in jail last year for supplying cannabis oil to a family friend to ease their baby's pain.

PHON and the X team succumbed to bullshit lobbying from attorney-general George Brandis's office, and health minister Greg Hunt's office. Senator James McGrath interrupted my Senate speech supporting the Greens to table a two-page letter from Hunt that convinced Senator Xenophon to back the government.

They also tried to sway me before the vote by claiming their opposition was solely to protect local growers! Why not allow the imports until local growers meet demand and then change the law again?

This is the same government that blocked a genuine plan to grow medicinal marijuana on Norfolk Island the way Tasmania grows policed opium poppies. There was also a claim that imported hemp would bring in a dangerous fungus, which, I've since been told, is the same one sometimes seen on rockmelons in the local greengrocers.

This fight has just begun. I pledge to bring back a private member's bill within six months, and I hope, by then, at least one of Hanson or Xenophon's teams will have found the spine to support us.

———————

What's in a name? I've been travelling around the country as a member of the National Integrity Commission Senate committee inquiry. We've been holding public hearings in Sydney, Brisbane and Melbourne, and hosting private meetings with the Crime and Corruption Commission, Independent Commission Against Corruption (ICAC) and Independent Broad-based Anti-Corruption Commission, and parliamentary overseeing committees, in all three cities, as we head for an August deadline on a national ICAC report.

I don't intend to canvass committee business here but it's no secret that witnesses have been suggesting names. NICAC (National Independent Anti-Corruption Commission). FICAC (Federal Independent Anti-Corruption Commission). Or, simply, NIC (National Integrity Commission).

It brought back two memories. When the commission to oversee integrity issues in Victoria Police was being formed, they came within a whisker of calling it the Police Integrity Group. Until somebody twigged on the acronym PIG. Think about it.

And when I was New York bureau chief for Fairfax, the GM sent me a memo advising that we were about to launch a new national weekly and asking did I have any suggestions for a name.

I remember responding: 'Dear Mr Falkingham. I suggest you call the new national weekly The National Weekly.' They called it the *National Times*.

And when Kerry Packer decided to change the *Women's Weekly* to a monthly mag, I suggested it should be called the *Women's Monthly*. After all, it is a periodical.

THE PERILS OF PAULINE

25 May 2017

Let's get one thing straight. If I had a tape apparently showing Liberal or Labor senators and apparatchiks ripping off their own candidates—not to mention the taxpayer, through the electoral commissioner—I'd be screaming bloody murder.

The fact that it was Pauline Hanson and James Ashby was, perhaps, more predictable (after the *Four Corners* report and the One Nation plane scandal) but still a major news story. Especially with the Queensland state election looming. What happened to 'keep the bastards honest'?

The Brisbane *Courier-Mail*, which broke the yarn, had two damning front pages. The first: 'Let's Make Some Cash. Exclusive: Hanson's top adviser recorded discussing scheme to rip off taxpayers and One Nation candidates'.

The follow-up was just as bad: 'Come Clean Pauline. Please explain. Secret recording challenges Hanson's claim on scheme'.

I won't detail the whole grubby scenario, but here's the potted version.

Hanson, Ashby and two other (unidentified) One Nation executives had a two-hour meeting late last year, and somebody recorded it.

Ashby said: 'Can I just point out, I've said this once before, there is an opportunity for us to make some money out of this, if we play it smart. Now I know they say you can't make money out of state elections, but you can. And I'll deny I ever said this, but …'

His plan, now dismissed by PHON as 'brainstorming', was to buy corflutes (those plastic posters of candidates for fences and lamp posts) for five dollars, sell them to their own One Nation candidates for eleven dollars and pocket the difference.

Then Ashby goes further, and this is why I said on radio they could face criminal charges of conspiring to defraud the taxpayer through the Queensland Electoral Commission.

He details how the candidates would submit an invoice to the commission for the inflated price, they would be reimbursed eleven dollars, keep five dollars and the rest would go to HQ.

Ashby: 'Where are we making money? 'Cause when you lodge the receipt, at the full price, with the Electoral Commission of Queensland, you get back the full amount that's been issued to you as an invoice.'

Hanson says on the tape (which I have heard): 'The candidates get something and the party gets a certain amount.'

At a weird presser in Perth, where it looked like the main protagonist was 'Senator' Ashby and Hanson was his sidekick, she stressed: 'Don't forget, I was at the meeting as well. You do not have the full recording of that meeting, so you have no idea what was said at the rest of the meeting. We knocked it on the head at the meeting. It didn't go ahead, that's why. It was an issue that was raised and it was knocked on the head there and then.'

A very reliable One Nation source, who provided me with the tape, questioned whether that was the complete truth.

Hanson says on the tape, 'Just look at it, what is the best financial outlook for us?'

But wait, there's more. The other woman at the meeting was worried about the financial health of some candidates. She said, 'But these candidates up front don't have a lot of money.'

Ashby had a slick solution: 'We'll sell it again to them for eight bucks.' Again?

And this damning kicker: 'Like what we did.'

What does that mean? I don't know, but it prompted me to tweet: *Hanson/Ashby tape transcript has JA saying poor* *candidates could be slugged $8 not $11. 'Like what we did'. Which mugs stung in past?*

———————

Some belated budget after-party gossip with the emphasis on 'sip'. On budget night I saw a blonde sipping red wine through a straw. I thought it must be some trendy new Canberra practice.

It brought back memories of the time when it was considered de rigueur, in the hobnob marquees at the Melbourne Cup, for socialites, in little dresses and big headgear, to sip a piccolo of French champagne through a straw—until they realised it got them shickered and unseemly much faster than a glass of pinot. (A doctor explained to me that the straw concentrates the bubbles, and the alcohol gets into your bloodstream much quicker. Sounds feasible.)

Curious, I asked the blonde why she did it and she gave me a plausible explanation: it meant she didn't smear her lipstick on the glass, and she was being considerate of the glass-washing barman and other patrons because everyone hates washing wineglasses with lipstick stains glued to them.

I recounted the story to a cynical female staffer. Bullbleep, she said. The woman was obviously heavily Botoxed, and with lips full of that stuff you can't feel the glass, and risk the wine missing your mouth.

Like when you try to navigate a glass of water after you've been to the dentist.

I wonder if Nicole Kidman drinks wine through a straw?

ONE DOWN, MANY MORE TO GO

1 June 2017

To steal from immigration minister Peter Dutton and his wishful thinking about the ABC, 'One down, many more to go.'

I am applying the quote to the passport ban on the 20 000 men (and a few women) on the child sex offender register, announced this week by foreign affairs minister Julie Bishop and justice minister Michael Keenan.

After the changes to the *Passports Act* are introduced into the House of Reps next month (and, hopefully, passed by the Senate) it will trigger what Bishop has called 'the biggest passport recall since Federation'. I have written and talked about it in detail before.

———————

I mentioned earlier that Anthony Foster, a great Australian, had died suddenly, only a few days after sitting in my Melbourne office with his wife, Chrissie, from whom he was inseparable, discussing how we could keep the government honest on the national redress scheme after the royal commission brings down its final report in December.

When you were with them, you forgot the horrors they had been through. Daughters Emma and Katie were raped by Catholic priest Father Kevin O'Donnell at Sacred Heart Catholic primary school. Emma killed herself in 2008 after years of mental and physical pain. And Katie was hit by a car after a drinking binge and is now brain-damaged and in a wheelchair and needing 24/7 care.

This couple, possessed of extraordinary strength and determination, fought the Catholic hierarchy for decades. They were mocked and disbelieved by church authorities, including Cardinal George Pell, whom Foster would describe as showing a 'sociopathic lack of empathy' for their anguish.

I applaud Victorian premier Dan Andrews for granting a state funeral for one of the most magnificent people I have ever met.

As the damning drip-drip feed of One Nation taped conversations digs deeper holes for Pauline Hanson and James Ashby (or Cashby, as the *Courier Mail* dubbed him) I'll just repeat my tweet from earlier in the week: *Senator Hanson: Please ex-plane!*

I got into Twitter scalding water when I observed that, on the queen's laudable hospital visit to young victims of the Manchester Arena bombing, it looked like she had *borrowed her orange hat from Willie Wonka's chocolate factory*.

What seemed to go unnoticed was her question to a teenager about whether she enjoyed the Ariana Grande concert.

It reminded me of the question supposedly asked of Mrs Lincoln at Ford's Theatre after her husband's assassination: 'But other than that, Mrs Lincoln, how did you like the play?'

Which gives me a segue into another presidential story. To get there, I have to mention Dasher. Senator Sam Dastyari is obsessed with hair—his own and mine.

In a filibustering effort in the Senate recently, he went on at length about how they couldn't all have perfect hair 'like

Senator Hinch over there'. And when our paths cross in the corridor, he'll ask: 'It's still perfect. Who's your hairdresser?'

Which leads me into a President John Kennedy story concerning his famous boyish head of hair. (He did follow eight years of the chrome-domed septuagenarian Dwight 'Ike' Eisenhower.)

In the flood of magazine colour stories about JFK and Jackie Kennedy in the 1960 presidential race against Tricky Dicky Nixon, I remember seeing one about Kennedy's hair. I was sixteen at the time and just started my career as a cub reporter on the *Taranaki Herald* (circulation 11 000) in New Plymouth, New Zealie.

Kennedy attributed his abundance of active follicles to the fact that he vigorously massaged his scalp for two minutes in the shower every morning while shampooing his mop. Ever since, I've taken that advice.

Useless fact: In April 1968, a new musical featuring nudity and hippies opened at the Biltmore Theatre on Broadway. I couldn't be bothered going and gave away my free tickets. It was a hit musical called *Hair*. I missed the dawning of the Age of Aquarius. Even though I was one.

FROM WATERGATE TO WATERMARK

8 June 2017

Forty-five years ago, there was Watergate and, more recently, closer to home, we had Choppergate—the 'gate' appendage being tagged on to any political scandal around the globe. I guess I'd be stretching it if I coined Watermarkgate. But, jeez, I'm tempted.

Watermark is the name of the Townsville restaurant where Pauline Hanson's resident Svengali, James Ashby, was holding court with PHON staff on 21 December last year—getting into the Christmas spirit, with a state election looming in WA, and the Hansonites predicting a swag of lower house seats and eight or nine upper house possies over there.

At the Water(mark)gate, Mr Ashby, as is his wont, was showing off a tad. He'd just announced to the team that the phone call he'd hung up on was from the attorney-general, Senator George Brandis. And Georgie Porgie had said, 'It's official, Culleton is out.' (This was WA One Nation senator Rod Culleton, on whom the High Court, sitting as the Court of Disputed Returns, would hand down its adverse verdict on 3 February.)

I'm told they all refilled their glasses and cheered.

At the marathon Senate estimates hearings recently, I asked Senator Brandis: 'Can you explain why James Ashby, at the Watermark restaurant in Townsville on December 21, according to people who were at the table, received a call from you. After he hung up he said: "That was Brandis, it's official, Culleton is out".'

Brandis said he didn't recall that conversation: 'But I do not dispute it either.'

He said he had a firm opinion of the likely outcome and would have told it to anyone who asked. If Ashby had asked, he would have told him too. So what?

I continued: 'People who were there make it sound like this wasn't just Senator Brandis Attorney-General's opinion; this was official that you knew Culleton was gone and you were passing it on to One Nation. Do you recall the phone call with Ashby at the Watermark in 21 December?'

Brandis said he didn't dispute Ashby was at the Watermark, but he didn't know that he was on the phone to him there.

'Was Ashby just showing off when he said it was Brandis on the phone?'

Brandis said he didn't know where he was that day.

My reply: 'I'm surprised you weren't at the Watermark.'

Brandis/Ashby. Personal phone calls. A fascinating liaison.

———————

This is not, currently, a popular opinion: I actually like Malcolm Turnbull. I think he is an honest and decent man. I don't think he has the gladiatorial skills of Tony Abbott or Bill Shorten in their blood sports.

On the same-sex marriage debate, I'd say: Malcolm, you promised a plebiscite (which you really never personally agreed with) and took it to a federal election. The Senate knocked you back. And I am proud that mine was a deciding vote that put the kybosh on a $250 million, $400 million, bitter, non-binding PR exercise.

When John Howard ambushed Australia in 2004—and tightened our laws to make sure marriage only applied to men and women (and foreign-certified same-sex unions were null and void here)—he made a big deal out of the fact it was parliament's job to rule on this. Not the courts, not the electorate. The parliament should do its elected job. And we should again.

Let's hope it happens at this sitting of parliament.

———————

Having praised the PM, let me now kick him. Before prime ministers and presidents (especially Turnbull and Trump) start mouthing off, they should get their facts right. After a fatal siege in Brighton, Melbourne, Turnbull attacked weaknesses in the Victorian parole system.

Let me get phlegmatic here. The killers of Masa Vukotic and Mersina Halvagis should not have been freed. And Adrian Bayley should have had his parole revoked long before he killed Jill Meagher. But the parole system in Victoria has tightened dramatically.

I believe the Melbourne-siege killer, having earlier been acquitted over a terrorist plot to attack the Holsworthy Army Base, but still on a watch list, should have been deported after having been training and fighting in Somalia. No question.

Why have at least forty men been allowed to return to Australia after fighting in the Middle East and not faced treason charges? Only two have been charged—as the government reluctantly told us last week.

David Hicks fought with the Taliban, boasted about his links with Osama bin Laden and ended up in Guantanamo. Why should returning ISIS fighters not face the same treatment here?

And something else that really disturbed me this week: why was the innocent woman taken hostage in the Melbourne siege treated with such disdain? Ignored by our leaders, she had a night of terror. Was she not mentioned because she was a prostitute?

———

After a shit week—Manchester, London, Melbourne: such horror, such sadness—may I end on a positive note. Dig out Ariana Grande's rendition of 'Somewhere over the Rainbow' from the tribute to terror victims on the other side of the world. It will moisten your eyes.

CARDIGANS ARE NOT PRIME MINISTERIAL

15 June 2017

Frankly, I don't give a Flying Finkel about the current emissions debate, until the government presents me—as a crucial crossbencher—with some genuine legislation they seriously think they can get through the Senate. And bring prices down.

I thought opposition leader Bill Shorten's weekend comments sounded conciliatory and, naively, I thought he and Malcolm Turnbull could find some common (50%–42%) common ground. Jeez, they've done this climate-warming dance before. And ended up going home alone.

It made me feel so warm and fuzzy and able to compromise that on the flight Shorten and I shared from Melbourne I could even ignore his ghastly blue woollen old-man's sweater, with a neck zipper, which accentuated his man boobs. The ones that starred in the 2016 election. (We did discuss his macho jogging article in *Men's Health*, or some such mag, where he did a Rocky run-up-the-steps thing.)

Chloe, you have style. You ooze class. My ex-wife used to stay with your mum at Yarralumla. How could you let him out of the house dressed like that? On the Queen's Birthday? I'm a republican, but ... what the?

I suggest that if you really want your man to inhabit the Lodge after the next election (which seems increasingly likely), you should google the cardigan Jimmy Carter wore for a televised fireside chat when he was president of the US of A.

That cardie made Jimmy, the peanut man, an un-re-electable prez.

John Blackman, Melbourne radio funny man, voice of Dickie Knee—and master of the single entendre—used the line 'When there's nothing left to be said, Derryn will still be saying it.'

It's a line I thought of earlier this year during the endless public hearings and Senate filibustering over 18C. And it applied last month, and this week, to the Greens before, finally, necessary amendments were made to the *Native Title Act*. To bastardise Churchill: never was so little said over such a long time by so few.

———————

Speaking of time wasting. In question time this week I asked attorney-general George Brandis whether the government had put on the agenda of the next Council of Australian Governments meeting my demand for a national public register of convicted sex offenders. And if not, why not?

And my supplementary question was: 'Why do we have pointless supplementary questions, especially laboriously written Dorothy Dixers? And will you support a Senate Reform Committee proposal to abolish them—as in the other place?'

President Stephen Parry ruled it out of order as not being relevant and offered me a second bite at it.

My response: 'And to prove my earlier point I waive this follow-up supplementary question.'

———————

Last week I wrote:

Dig out Ariana Grande's rendition of 'Somewhere over the Rainbow' from the tribute to terror victims on the other side of the world. It will moisten your eyes.

I have the same reaction to the version of this, and the segue into 'What a Wonderful World', by Hawaiian legend Israel Kamakawiwo'ole.

It gives me a 'rainbow' segue into two serious political issues. I have said that I believe Malcolm Turnbull has to 'do a Gough' and crash through or crash.

He must kick the Abbotts and Abetzes and Christensens right in the gonads over climate change. He and ScoMo have to have the balls to say: 'This is the new troika. Suck it up or fuck off.'

Turnbull must allow a vote on same-sex marriage this year. Just … get … it … done. You honoured your pledge to take a plebiscite to the election—to appease the Abbotteers. Even though you didn't want a plebiscite.

You got it through 'the other place' and got defeated in the Senate. We saved your Mother Hubbard treasurer between $250 million and $400 million, and I am honoured that my 'no' vote helped kill the plebiscite.

Follow John Howard's advice when he tightened the *Marriage Act* (with Labor's craven support) in 2004 to cement man-woman-only marriage and ban foreign same-sex marriage recognition. He said it was up to the elected politicians to do their job. Not the courts. Not the populace.

Which brings me back to my 'Over the Rainbow' comment.

I have this (unchallenged … yet) theory about the gay community's embrace of the rainbow as their symbol. And I'll ignore Abetz's conspiratorial theories about the origin.

The song was written for the movie *The Wizard of Oz* by Yip Harburg in 1939. And sung by child star Judy Garland.

Flash forward thirty years and I am in a Broadway theatre. Judy Garland is on stage. Gay guys are throwing flowers at her, like Dame Edna with her gladdies in reverse.

Judy Garland was one of the original, self-proclaimed 'fag hags' and it wasn't just due to Dorothy's ruby red shoes. Later, in Australia, maybe it was because her son-in-law, for a while, was Peter Allen, the boy from Oz who went to Rio.

And decades later than that, who could have thunk it that the bloke writing this diary would appear on *Dancing with the Stars* in full boy from Oz ruffles. Doing the full maracas number on national TV—with his fly undone.

… stranger than fiction.

WHICH LABOR MPS INTIMIDATE THE COALITION IN QUESTION TIME?

22 June 2017

One morning I cried in 'the other place', as the supposedly superior Senate dwellers are forced to call it.

I was privileged to be seated in the VIP section of the House of Reps when—as Julian Lennon would say—saltwater welled in my eyes.

The occasion was foreign affairs minister Julie Bishop introducing into the house my amendments to the passport laws to ban 20 000 men (and a few women) on the convicted child sex offenders register from travelling overseas. The bill had sailed through the Senate. I said there:

> I know there are Australian deviates right here using their credit cards and Skype for real-time sex crimes.

I was given evidence today of a paedophile hiring a baby from her mother in the Philippines for less than $100 for his real-time gratification on Skype. The baby was three months old. So, I'll be working closely in the months ahead with a group called IJM, the International Justice Mission Australia, to fight cybersex trafficking in our region. I stand here tonight, a very proud man and very proud of you all, in both houses, for rescuing hundreds, thousands, of children from a truly evil and depraved culture.

———————

Keen as mustard, as they say, I was the first person into the house that morning (after the green-jacketed attendants) and was ushered to a prime position next to an open door where Liberal Party MPs had gathered for their morning pre-sitting strategy gabfest—which I eavesdropped on, to discover was a pep talk from Mr Fixit, the 'election-winning machine', Christopher Pyne.

I reckon his rev-up to the team could have given Ron Barassi a run for his money: 'You've got to be noisy in there. Really noisy. Don't be intimidated by [Chris] Bowen and [Joel] Fitzgibbon.'

It reminded me of that motto from the *Hinch* program: 'If you are being run out of town, pretend it's a parade and you're leading it.'

———————

Speaking of 'the other place', every morning in the Senate, we all gather for prayers and the tribute to Aboriginal elders 'past and present'. As an atheist, I stare at the vaulted ceiling during the God bit. So do most of the Greens and some ALP senators. Senator Malcolm Roberts cups his hands skyward in supplication (I assume he has empirical evidence of a higher being). And senators Barry O'Sullivan and Matt Canavan do the traditional 'spectacles, testicles, watch and wallet' routine with the sign of the cross.

What shocked me, on that visit to the other place, was that the opposition didn't turn up for the opening ceremony. I thought their caucus meeting had run over time. Somebody doing a Pyne-style rev-up. But the PM, and several ministers, told me that they rarely do show up. Harmless Westminster pomp. Bit sad, really.

Even though a newbie in Foggy Bottom, I have already experienced those adrenaline-filled highs and morale-sapping lows. And that's how it played out last week.

The passport-ban high evaporated that same afternoon when, in a true act of bastardry, One Nation senator Brian Burston blocked my attempt to introduce a motion for a joint parliamentary watchdog committee to make sure the national redress scheme gets real compensation for victims identified in the sex abuse royal commission.

One Nation tried to block it again this week but lost. Burston told other senators it was 'payback' but also said I was only wanting to claim the committee chairman's spot because I was greedy and wanted the $21 000 allowance that came with it.

The following morning, after prayers, I was given rare permission to refute his defamatory claims that I was 'in it for the money as committee chairman'.

I announced if there were a fee I would donate it all to the Wintringham project for housing homeless people over fifty.

To be honest, I was surprised how emotional I got in that one minute on my feet, but nobody likes to be accused of exploiting vulnerable kids.

———

This bad blood extended to the corridors and a crossbench committee meeting, which I chaired. The One Nation grinch said, 'I haven't finished with you yet, you grub.' I'll concede I did greet him with 'You're a bastard, Burston.' I thought it quite alliterative.

———

You have spoken. Channel Seven ran a poll on whether or not Australians support my call for a national public register of sex offenders. Yes: 94%. Fear vigilantes: 6%. Nearly 200 000 have signed my petition. Thanks, Australia.

A MOST APOCRYPHAL BLOWJOB

29 June 2017

In a frantic wheeler-dealer week of Senate sittings, with one marathon session lasting about sixteen hours straight, things tended to get a tad delusional.

But even allowing for that, a swag of politicians (including the prime minister) were wondering how the hell Hinch could get Neil Armstrong and the moon landing into the Gonski debate.

It happened. Here's how Hansard recorded my concluding comments, as I supported the much-amended 'Gonski 2.0 Plus', as the colluding crossbenchers dubbed it: 'And before I sit down, to steal from Neil Armstrong's apocryphal story about what he really said when he walked on the moon: "Good luck, Mr Gonski!"'

Since then, I've had a heap of Hansonesque 'Please explain?'s.

My meaning was too salacious to detail in a publicly broadcast daytime Senate speech.

The 'Good luck, Mr Gonski' was a steal of 'Good luck, Mr Gorsky!'—which Armstrong reportedly said on the moon.

He did not say it. But an urban myth, believed by millions and googled to death, is that NASA censured the Apollo 11 astronaut's historic words as he stepped out of the lunar lander, *Eagle*, and walked on the moon.

The conspiracy theorists claim he actually said, 'That's one small step for man, one giant leap for mankind—and good luck, Mr Gorsky.'

So, who the hell was Mr Gorsky? And why wish him luck from outer space?

For the believers, I will explain.

When Neil Armstrong was growing up in Wapakoneta, Ohio, he lived next door to Mr and Mrs Gorsky. One day, he kicked his ball over the fence. It landed under their open bedroom window.

Neil clambered over the fence to retrieve it and, as the future astronaut picked it up, heard Mrs Gorsky say: 'A blowjob? Listen, I'll give you a blowjob when that skinny kid next door walks on the moon.'

Good luck, Mr Gorsky.

It's not true … but it's now referenced in Hansard.

———————

The commentators, and the Twitterati, had predictable fun as parliament adjourned for the long winter break. We're all going off on 'free junkets to Europe', and that image wasn't helped by the announcement that we're also getting a pay rise.

My 'junket' will be as part of a parliamentary delegation going with Save the Children to Lebanon and refugee camps in Jordan, near the Syrian border. I'll report on it later, but this gives me a segue into the greatest put-down I think I've ever been given. And it involved Save the Children.

About thirty-five years ago, Ron Walker, former lord mayor of Melbourne, invited me to go to the Sudan to look at the work STC was doing in Africa. The invite was spurred by reports I'd done for 3AW after travelling to the barren Gujarat state in India with Community Aid Abroad. An added incentive was the promise of a rare interview with Princess Anne, who would be there for Save the Children.

On the last day of the trip, after hours of bouncing around in a Jeep in a dusty wadi near the Mali border, I scored the exclusive interview with the princess that her staff had been avoiding. (When I got it, I was grilled by a pissed-off Fleet Street mob. My response: 'I give good letter.' On our last night, I had peeled off from the group, gone back to my shack and bashed out a personal note, which I slipped to her aide-de-camp the next morning.)

Late afternoon, HRH emerged alone from a straw-roofed mud hut in the middle of nowhere. I launched into my first question: 'Your Royal Highness, as Patron of Save the Children, what do you think—'.

She cut me off with a glare of Julie Bishop-level intensity. 'I am not the patron … Mother is.' Anne was only the president.

It seemed appropriate that, at that very moment, a donkey hee-hawed in the background.

It's true. We caught it on the bulky old Nagra tape recorder.

Back to the real world of Canberra politics. I know bullshit is breakfast in the national capital. But this pious Bill Shorten Gonski tweet was really hard to stomach: *A Prime Minister in touch with regular people wouldn't cut billions from schools, and a Prime Minister who does will not last long.*

It prompted my reply: *Bill. Your own insiders are saying the deal the crossbenchers achieved with secret Greens help is great. You just can't admit that.*

Penny Wong and Labor had George Brandis on Senate toast last week, and they blew it. They argued that the government was in disarray and forcing messy legislation through.

Senators George Brandis and Mitch Fifield were playing funny buggers, to extend sitting hours to force a decision on Gonski, and Labor, quite legitimately, tore the government apart on cynically playing time games so as to sit late and filibuster Gonski through the upper house.

But Labor missed a doozy.

I called a point of order. Why? Brandis put his ponderous notice of motion with points 1a and 3a but missed 2a. Sloppy. And nobody picked it up. Old subeditors never die.

TIME FOR THE REAL TURNBULL

13 July 2017

He was the headline writers' dream—and great cartoon fodder—as he danced on the Libs' policy hot coals: Malcolm in the middle/in a muddle, etc.

If he'd stuck to the middle, as he is now saying Menzies always envisaged for his party, prime minister Malcolm Turnbull would, I believe, be looking healthier in the polls.

It was the job-protecting lurch into the narrow, vindictive, divisive ultra-right wing world of Tony Abbott, and Eric Abetz and Kevin Andrews and George Christensen, that made thousands of voters who had applauded his ascendancy decide that that emperor had no clothes.

It is no exaggeration to say that there was a genuine feeling of excitement, close to adulation, when Turnbull toppled Abbott. Many liberal Liberals, middle-grounders and some Labor voters thought here was a clever, intelligent, successful businessman occupying the Lodge. And a republican to boot. And an advocate of same-sex marriage. A political match made in heaven for many voters.

Okay, he looked like a candidate from Central Casting, but was that so bad? He didn't eat raw onions or walk like he'd just got off a horse.

The history rewriters forget that after Abbott had thirty-nine dissenters in that February 2015 'empty chair' leadership challenge, even some of his current boosters were calling him a 'dead man walking'—so on the nose, he was not re-electable.

And now his successor is halfway to the number of bad public opinion polls that he (rashly) used as a major reason for ousting his predecessor.

I have written before that, for Turnbull, it is past time for a Gough-ian crash through or crash. And the best way to start it is to just get out of the way. Let the Dean Smith same-sex marriage bill take to the field. (I not only offered Smith my support, I offered to co-sponsor his bill if he needed me.)

Give your government tribe a conscience vote in 'the other place'. It would fly through the Senate, could be law by the end of August, and Neil Diamond's 'September Morn' could be playing at same-sex weddings all over Australia. Within weeks.

Malcolm, at least you'd be remembered as someone doing something positive. For triggering something that 75 per cent of Australians want. You might even get invited back to the Gay and Lesbian Mardis Gras next year.

Unless, of course, the right wingers' rumours are true—that to get the numbers to replace Abbott, you sold your soul to the Nats with a guarantee never to abandon a plebiscite. Maybe it was even in writing.

———————

Unlike The Donald, I can stay away from Twitter, and I have regarding the Pell court saga. I'm glad to see he has returned to Australia to face charges and 'have my day in court'. (The Vatican sanctuary story was a furphy.) The only time I have tweeted about it was to say: *Been trying to stay out of this but: Predictable stuff from Pell PR teams like Bolt and Devine. Don't insult genuine responsible jurors.* They conveniently ignore the fact that the High Court ruled the opposite in the Father Glennon case: that Glennon would receive a fair trial despite media reports of previous convictions. I should know that; they were my media reports about that child rapist that prompted the High Court decision.

Which leads me to that book: *Cardinal: The Rise and Fall of George Pell.*

Louise Milligan's book has rightly been withdrawn from sale by Melbourne University Publishing, pending Pell's trial. I took a copy to Thailand for a relaxing reading break, and it was the least relaxing holiday read I could have packed.

This book is one of the most forensic, explosive, historically detailed tomes I have ever read. The publishers, MUP, were brave to get it out there. This, and Pell's trial, will make the final royal commission report vital, viral reading. And then I'm chairing a joint parliamentary committee into the national redress scheme, to make sure the churches and other institutions pay the victims compensation for what they condoned or ignored.

That pug-nosed American actor Karl Malden used to spruik the American Express card on telly and earnestly warn us to 'never leave home without it'.

In recent years, I've felt that way about my laptop. Wouldn't/couldn't leave the apartment without it. And that's surprising, since I used to be one of those technologically dyslexic fogeys who didn't know what @ or dot.com meant and thought Microsoft was a new upgrade of Sorbent toilet paper.

Last week, I did the unthinkable. I went to Thailand on vacation and forgot my laptop. Karl Malden, your words didn't apply. It was bliss.

THOSE DUELLING DUAL SENATORS

19 July 2017

If it was politically surreal to watch Scott Ludlam call a presser in Perth on Friday to announce his resignation from the Senate because he held dual citizenship, how the hell do you categorise Larissa Waters following suit a few days later?

For Ludlam, there were almost inconsequential throwaway lines, as—in 24-carat Greenie fashion—he revealed that (aw shucks; sorry, folks) he'd never really been a senator. Dual citizenship with Kiwiland and all that. Bloody section 44.

It's hard to believe that Ludlam—he of the neat hair, colourful socks and expensive shoes—would have become the third non-senator to be forced to fall on his rusty sword this 45th parliament. He joined One Nation's Rod Culleton— whom I warned on Twitter, before the 2 July election, would not pass muster—and Family First's Bob Day. ('Senator' Ludlam's public mockery of Day's technical sloppiness will no doubt be framed by somebody.)

And now Queensland Green (and, like Ludlam, a Greens deputy leader in the Senate) Larissa Waters has been forced, for passport reasons, to pull the plug.

Around the Ludlam exit, the rumours swirled about other foreign-born members and senators. Waters (born in Canada) another Green, Peter Whish-Wilson (born in Singapore), PHON's Malcolm Roberts (born in India), Hinch (born across the ditch), Labor's Sam Dastyari (born in Iran) and the Libs' Eric Abetz (born in Germany).

And there were serious doubts about Bob Day's replacement, Kenyan-born Lucy Gichuhi. Did her failure to reapply for Kenyan citizenship constitute a renunciation after she arrived here in 1999?

Following the Ludlam bombshell, other ripples spread. I tweeted: *The Ludlam dual citizenship resignation should re-ignite the Tony Abbott dual citizenship debate. When did he renounce Britain?*

A Queensland terrier, blogger Tony Magrathea, had been chasing an Abbott answer for years, and he'd enlisted Labor's Terri Butler.

Suspicions were further fuelled by the fact that Abbott wouldn't respond to freedom of information requests, the PM's office was saying documents were not available, and then the files were sealed.

I did email the dogged Magrathea and point out that, in my experience in current affairs, most conspiracies turned out to be fuck-ups.

The Ludlam mess prompted former PM Abbott to answer the 'rumour mongers' last week by tweeting a copy of a letter from the Poms, showing he had renounced his British citizenship in 1993.

(And that prompted questions about how in the 1980s he could get a foreign student's scholarship to Oxford as an Australian while holding a British passport.)

———

The Ludlam mess raises more questions than he has answered. There was a change.org petition circulated three years ago, demanding the Greens deputy leader answer the dual citizenship question. Why did that not at least set off some alarm bells?

It again raises the sloppy issue of ineligible candidates. I believe all would-be politicians who were born overseas should be compelled to provide documented proof of dual citizenship renunciation to the AEC at the same time as their nomination form and fee. And why haven't their parties, large and small, policed it? I heard the Greens leader, senator

Richard Di Natale, saying this week they were having a 'root and branch' review of what should have been bleeding obvious.

I must admit I did tweet: *And now Senator Waters. Seems Greens should have spent less time hugging trees and more time crossing Ts.*

As it turns out, Scott Ludlam's exposure as a sham senator could be the result of collateral damage. The Perth barrister who did it was a constitutional law buff who actually had another ex-Kiwi in his sights: me.

According to the *Weekend Australian*, John Cameron—a lawyer, not a political junkie—applied to the archives across the ditch for info on several senators.

> I checked about three weeks ago with the NZ Department of Internal Affairs and applied to search the register in relation to Mr Ludlam and Senator Hinch. I expected the human headline may not have done it and Mr Ludlam would have done it, but it was the other way around. I received the certificate for Mr Ludlam which showed he was still a citizen but for Mr Hinch the certificate shows that he renounced his citizenship before the last election.

Postscript: The luckiest man in all this is that conservative stickler for rules and regulations, Senator Eric Abetz. Stickler, except maybe when they apply to him.

Abetz held dual citizenships until he renounced his German citizenship. One report claimed that was on 9 March 2010.

That would mean he was illegally a senator when he was elected in 1994, 1998 and 2004. But Jennifer Bechwati from Sky News tweeted that Abetz renounced his German citizenship in 1974.

Tasmanian art dealer John Hawkins, who has just dropped a High Court challenge to Abetz's eligibility, might want to look at the issue again.

CAN ANYBODY SAVE THESE CHILDREN?

31 July 2017

Five days ago, I was five miles from the Syrian border. We had an armed escort, even though after five days of fierce fighting, Hezbollah had just forced the surrender of militants (formerly aligned with al-Qaeda) near the town in Lebanon we were visiting with Save the Children (STC).

The area we were in is on the Australian government's official no-go list for tourists, but I was there as part of a parliamentary delegation with STC, who were keen to show us where Australian foreign aid for refugees is going in the Middle East. Not only through STC but other NGOs like CARE and PLAN and Caritas and Oxfam and the World Food Programme and the United Nations refugee agency. We visited them all in a whirlwind week. And I saw the wonderful work they are all doing, especially with vulnerable kids.

Just to show you the complexities of Lebanese politics: last week, the Lebanese army sat back, behind a line they had drawn at a nearby disputed ancient road, while Hezbollah ran their own race, so to speak. Hezbollah, a banned foreign military force—proscribed as a terrorist organisation by the United States and Australia—was there, successfully fighting a war for Lebanon, on Lebanese soil.

(I should explain that, in a recent and Machiavellian political coup, Hezbollah has been brought into the strange coalition that makes up the formula supposedly leading to well-overdue elections in Lebanon. But I'll leave that to the Middle East experts to decipher.)

To further confuse you, as Hezbollah forced the white flag from Jabhat Fateh al-Sham (formerly known as al-Nusra Front) and allowed the militants safe passage to Syria in exchange for the return of captured Lebanese soldiers, the Lebanese army was preparing its own assault on a few hundred Daesh (also known as Islamic State or ISIS) militants holding border enclaves next to the nearby towns of Al-yup Qaa and Ras Baalbek.

That thrust could—just could—finally rid Lebanon of ISIS-associated militant groups and enhance border security for the first time in yonks. Check Al Jazeera for the latest.

Our week-long trip to Lebanon and Jordan included a visit to a 'non-city' of 80 000 Syrian refugees outside Amman and an illegal settlement of 700 refugees north of Beirut.

It showed us two countries with staggering humanitarian and economic problems, trying to solve the chronic situation in different ways and neither really succeeding. Frankly, I doubt there is an answer. Especially not in the foreseeable future.

In Jordan, they have two massive refugee cities. There are 80 000 people in the well-planned and well-run camp we visited at Zaatari, covering 8.5 square kilometres and divided into twelve distinct blocks. There's another more primitive one, with 55 000 Syrian refugees.

In Block One, Jordan welcomed 2000 Syrian refugees in 2012. Now, five years later, there are 80 000 residents. The border is now closed.

The authorities say the city is not permanent and even forbid the pouring of concrete. The families live in what they optimistically call caravans, but are really dongas, or shipping containers or primitive building-site huts.

While the Jordanian government tells the resentful people it is all temporary, there are power lines there—and the water pipes I saw being installed looked pretty permanent. Hinch's Hunch is that this 'city', one of Jordan's largest, will still be here twenty-five bleak years later.

In Lebanon, they are trying to learn from their previous problem, after they welcomed 400 000 Palestinians into their country years ago. They are all still there in one region.

The government decided there would be no such camps for the Syrian refugees who fled across a porous border after the civil war started in 2011. These new refugees would be urbanised.

The problem is there are now between 1 million and 1.5 million Syrian refugees in Lebanon, and they make up about 35 per cent of the population.

Imagine if Australia suddenly had an influx of 7 million refugees. That's the influx percentage that Lebanon is dealing with. Or trying to.

The unofficial camp I visited had 700 residents, most of them young kids. There are 2500 such camps across Lebanon. The authorities keep dismantling them and moving the refugees on because the local municipalities can't cope. The nomads then move to an even less inviting municipality and try to start again.

While we were in Lebanon, a fleet of trucks was driving around from municipality to municipality trying to unload tonnes of solid waste. Just imagine the sewage problems. I suspect most of it just goes into the supposedly pristine Mediterranean.

In both countries, there is hidden—but, I suspect, seeth-ing—resentment of the aid to refugees, by poor Lebanese and Jordanians. Actually, I know it is true there is. In the hours of briefings we had from various NGO officials they stressed how new programs for refugees also included the disadvan-taged in the host countries.

———————

Images I won't easily forget.

In Beirut, two refugee families (one ten people, one six) living in two rooms, without electricity, and being charged US$500 a month for the privilege. They get some charity dol-lars for food and medicine, but adults and kids go out and work (usually illegally) for a pittance.

In Amman, a mother tells me how her 5-year-old was killed by Assad's chemical warfare on his own people. 'We didn't know what it was. The doctors didn't know what it was. It was like a spider web …'

In a town near the Syrian border—so close to it we could see the parched, khaki-coloured, mountainous dividing line—I spent time with a bunch of refugee kids, aged between nine and sixteen, in a Save the Children safe house.

One case, in particular, will haunt me. A 9-year-old girl. Her innocent eyes emphasised by traditional Arabic kohl. She worked (illegally) sweeping up and cleaning at a hairdressing salon.

I thought that if current practices prevail, she'll be married to an adult male within five years.

The refugee crisis has caused the amount of child brides to rocket in both Jordan and Lebanon. Desperate families are sacrificing a daughter for the dowry, which also means one less mouth to feed.

In the crowded makeshift towns, where there is no privacy, fathers are also forcing their teenage daughters into arranged marriages to deter sexual harassment and, supposedly, save both their and the family's honour.

In Lebanon last week, humanitarian groups were lobbying politicians to try to overturn a custom under which the rapist of a child can avoid prosecution and any punishment if he agrees to marry his victim.

He gets off scot-free. She is condemned to a life of sexual abuse.

HE FINALLY SAID IT!

10 August 2017

I wrote it. I finally wrote it. 'Shame, shame, shame.' And I wasn't channelling Steve Vizard as Hunch.

After the Liberal lower house rebels folded (except for that Queensland croc, Warren Entsch) under threat of having their next preselection pulled, and the Libs decided to trundle out their discredited plebiscite again, I did tweet: *Shame, shame, shame. New Zealand, Ireland, Germany, Taiwan. All legalised same-sex marriage. Human decency. This Government disgusts me.*

Maybe 'disappoints me' would have been more couthful (as they say) but I did feel disgusted after Malcolm Turnbull and his party room robbed the parliament of our right to vote on legislation.

As I asked attorney-general Senator George Brandis, as the PM's man in the Senate, in question time—in my rare entitlement to even ask a question as a crossbencher:

> Former Liberal prime ministers John Howard and even Tony Abbott have said in the past that changes to the *Marriage Act* should be made by the elected representatives of the country. Even Prime Minister Menzies once promised discrimination would not be written into Australian marriage law. Why won't your government let us do our job?

Speaking of Menzies: it's hard to believe, as the Turnbull government again blocks a free vote on marital matters, that Ming, the so-called Liberal Moses, did just the opposite.

In the 'no fault' divorce debate in 1958, Menzies allowed a conscience vote and justified it by saying, '… as the question of divorce closely touches the individual conscience of members, we propose that, though it will be a government measure, it shall not be treated as a party measure. Therefore, honourable members will be in a position to discuss it according to their own lights and views.'

Wouldn't it have been wonderful to hear our self-styled 'strong leader', Malcolm Turnbull, borrow those words this week?

Has Pauline Hanson seen the empirical evidence proving that Senator Malcolm Roberts did not hold dual citizenship at the time he nominated for One Nation last year?

She says she has, but at a trainwreck media conference this week, she called the situation 'complicated' and 'a little bit more, can I say—it's not straightforward'.

Then Hanson announced she was moving a motion to have Roberts referred to the High Court sitting as the Court of Disputed Returns. (PHON tried to make it sound like a noble cause by dint of their 'transparent' referral but it should have been done the day before when senators Canavan, Waters and Ludlum's names were sent up.)

Along the way, Senator Hanson mangled Senator Dastyari's name and Senator (?) Roberts butchered that of former senator Larissa Waters.

Before the Senate endorsed the Roberts referral, I explained that I'd tried a different tack the day before.

I met with a number of my crossbench colleagues and with Greens leader Richard Di Natale. I also had a sit-down with Roberts. He told me that a statutory declaration had been provided to Senate president Stephen Parry, addressing the question of his eligibility under section 44. He even read me parts of that stat dec.

Roberts assured me that the claim he had travelled on a British passport was wrong. That he had travelled on his mother's Australian passport.

He said he was confident he had taken 'all reasonable steps' to confirm his sole Australian citizenship and that he had a QC's advice it would pass scrutiny in the High Court.

Following further information I received in the next twenty-four hours, I said, 'Well, I won't say the senator lied to me, I'll just say he was very economical with the truth.'

The major parties didn't exactly cover themselves with glory in all this. In our chat, Roberts said he would support a Greens motion to have all senators' credentials (his included) referred to an independent auditor under the auspices of the Legal and Constitutional Affairs Committee.

By the time it got to the vote, it had the support of the Greens, One Nation, the Xenophon Team, Hinch, Leyonhjelm and Gichuhi. The Libs, the Nats and the ALP all voted against it.

This was after the attorney-general had given an almost forelock-tugging (if he had one) defence of Roberts and warned us it was a grave thing to do and don't make a habit of it.

He was seen to shake Roberts's hand as he left the chamber.

———————

I'm on a Senate committee that is looking at long-overdue reforms to Senate procedures. Several of us want to cut speaking times from twenty minutes to fifteen minutes—like the limit in 'the other place'.

I'm also keen to get rid of the two supplementary follow-up questions in question time. Especially those excruciating Dorothy Dixers from government backbenchers.

So, when questioning the attorney-general about the refusal to allow a marriage equality vote, I framed my third question thus: 'Mr President, unlike in the other place, we get these time-wasting supplementary questions, especially Dorothy Dixers, I'll forfeit that time.'

———————

And the best Freudian slip of the year. Malcolm Roberts: 'I've always thought that I was British … that I was Australian.'

OF DOMINOES AND PICK-UP STICKS

17 August 2017

Some of you might remember those childhood games of dominoes and pick-up sticks. Jeez, I thought of them this week.

If that constitutional legal nerd, Perth lawyer John Cameron, hadn't decided a month ago to go after my antecedents, hadn't gone sniffing around in Wellington to see if I had renounced my Kiwi citizenship, the Turnbull government might not be in the 'deep doodoo' it is now. The dominoes might not have fallen. The sticks might not have moved.

Deputy prime minister and National Party leader Barnaby Joyce—aka Crocodile Dunedin—might have avoided being exposed as an All Black by descent. Come on down, Baa-naby (as many newspaper headline writers dubbed him this week)!

Greens leader Richard Di Natale told me, with some passion, this week, 'It's all your fault.'

You see, Cameron came after me. He got Greens deputy leader Scott Ludlam as collateral damage and then the rest of the dominoes started to fall.

So, queries about my citizenship (regarding which I proved to be one of the few responsible cleanskins) could bring down this shambolic, clumsy government.

Ludlam fell, then Larissa Waters failed scrutiny, and then Malcolm Roberts and then Barnyard Barnaby. And, in a desperate manoeuvre to muddy the waters, the usually astute and level-headed foreign minister, Julie Bishop, bowled underarm to New Zealand.

Then we saw really tawdry behaviour from the 'chief law officer in the land', as they call him, Senator George Brandis, as he tried to suspend standing orders to censure the opposition's leader in the Senate, and opposition foreign affairs spokeswoman, Penny Wong.

He accused her of 'inappropriate conduct'—pretty mild when words like 'treason' were being tossed around the other place—but he then alleged Wong had engaged 'in conduct which makes her unfit to ever hold the office of Foreign Minister of Australia'.

I invoked the ire of Senator Doug Cameron by announcing I would support the suspension of standing orders. He claimed that my support gave the defamatory Brandis motion credibility.

I pointed out that I will never gag debate in the chamber. And, as I told the Senate, I supported the government in trying (they failed) to get the issue to the floor, but had told Brandis in advance I would vote against a censure motion, which I considered a smokescreen for Barnaby Joyce's and the government's citizenship quagmire.

———

On the dual citizenship mess, there was a gaggle of strange bedfellows on the 'aye' side, voting in favour of a Greens motion to refer the dual citizenship question to the Legal and Constitutional Affairs Committee so that an independent auditor would examine every senator's validity on the question of citizenship schizophrenia.

Almost the entire crossbench—Greens, Hinch, Xenophon, One Nation, Lambie—voted for the referral.

The Libs, the Nationals and Labor, abetted by Leyonhjelm and new independent Gichuhi (who was born in Kenya), voted against such senatorial scrutiny.

———

A Twitter comment on the incompetent way this embattled government handled the embarrassing Baa-naby business: *Why didn't Turnbull and Joyce get this out on Fri or Sat? Why destroy another first day back? Suicidal oxygen starving.*

Earlier, as the PM doggedly, and I believe recklessly, held on to Joyce as a cabinet member and deputy PM, I tweeted: *So one National Senator Matt Canavan resigns from Cabinet, says he won't vote until High Court but Dep. PM. Joyce stays and will vote. Duh?*

(And a special mention of the troll who said a senator whose IQ is so low he uses a word like 'duh' is not fit to hold office. Funny thing is, I've never watched *The Simpsons*.)

Airport security has been in the news again lately, with the announcement of a super-duper homeland security department, with Peter Dutton as El Supremo.

It raises an issue that has bugged me for years. I have a reasonably recognisable face. At the airport check-in counter I diligently pull out ID with my photo on it.

But if I had checked in at a domestic terminal and just used the bag drop, I would have needed no proof of identification.

I could have checked in online with Fred Smith's stolen credit card and boarded the plane unchallenged.

It doesn't make sense.

THE RAINBOW CONNECTION

23 August 2017

As the Abbott family's war on same-sex marriage escalated on Twitter and 2GB this week (that's the Abbott, not Addams, Family), Peter van Onselen asked Anthony Albanese on Sky News where were the Labor politicians who oppose same-sex marriage. Why weren't they speaking out?

We had seen Bill Shorten and Victorian premier Dan Andrews flanked by rainbows in Melbourne over the weekend.

Albo reaffirmed that he was, and always will be, in favour of a conscience vote. But he ducked the real question: where were the Labor 'No' campaigners?

I think I can throw some light on the issue after something that happened in the Senate last week. The Xenophon Team's Senator Skye Kakoschke-Moore solicited my support, and that of the Greens, to cleverly tag a same-sex marriage amendment to another nuts-and-bolts technical bill that had the words 'Marriage Act' in it.

I believed Labor was on board too. Labor, Greens, X and Hinch—we were home.

It didn't happen. Labor withdrew support. Why? Because, according to Senate corridor rumours, four, five or even six Labor senators will vote 'No' in the postal survey—if it gets a High Court green light. And presumably they would later in the Senate, as well. You can use that, Peter.

———————

As the political dominoes kept falling, and Fiona Nash and Nick XenaPom joined Crocodile Dunedin in the High Court queue, probably the best Twitter line (for me) came from the bloke who tweeted that the way things were going, *the humanheadline will be PM in a few weeks.*

I must admit that tickled my fancy, as they used to say. Not because of any desire to take Troubled Turnbull's precarious job—but because so many major party nabobs had not done their homework.

Let's be blunt here. If a political greenhorn like me—with the Justice Party only officially registered with the AEC three months before the 2016 election and working with a handful of volunteers—could get my shit together and papers in order, why couldn't the big boys? Just assign one staffer to check on citizenship obligations.

Hey, I've been an Australian citizen for more than thirty-five years, but I read section 44 and knew what had to be done. And I did it. That's why this is a sympathy-free zone.

After Turnbull, Bishop, Brandis and Joyce conspired with Nash for her to do a 'dump and run' just before the Senate shut down last Thursday night (even though she knew the previous Monday that she was a UK citizen), I was, coincidentally, on an estimates hearing of the Legal and Constitutional Affairs Committee the next morning.

Most pollies had fled the capital, but Senator George Brandis had to be there as head of the attorney-general's department.

I can confess that Labor's Murray Watt, the Greens' Nick McKim and I ambushed committee chairman, the irascible Ian Macdonald, and forced a private committee meeting, literally in one of the Senate 'corridors of power', and got the Nash–Joyce section 44 issue on to the hearing agenda.

To be fair to the attorney-general, he signalled he was happy to answer questions on the issue.

The least Pauline Hanson could do would be to thank me. If I hadn't got the rules changed last year to let TV cameras and photographers record everything going on at any time in the Senate, the nation would not have seen her dramatic burlesque burqa entrance. Nor other senators' reactions.

Under ancient Senate rules, she would only have been recorded on film when she 'had the call' and stood to ask a question of attorney-general George Brandis.

You would have been robbed of seeing the standing ovation for Brandis from Labor, the Greens and the crossbench as president Stephen Parry futilely called for order. (And I'll have more on the burqa saga later.)

———————

Back to the dual citizenship schmozzle. To me, Bill Shorten looked stoopid on *Q&A* this week when asked by Tony Jones if he'd provide proof that he'd renounced his British-descent citizenship. To others he would have looked shady—a tag he's managed to shed since the royal commission spotlighted his union money-shuffling days.

Four or five times, Jones pushed the opposition leader, which concluded thus:

TJ: OK, let's just confirm this. You're not going to release the documents, is that right?

BS: Well, I know what I am, and the point is we have a screening process. I've been clear four times.

TJ: No but, just … so that's a no, you're not going to release the documents?

BS: What is the case to release it?

TJ: I'm just asking you.

Jeez. Even Barack Obama released his Hawaiian birth certificate to try to shut up the crazy birther movement over there. A nutty conspiracy theory cynically pushed along for years by the man who now occupies the White House.

BIGGEST HEALTH SCANDAL SINCE THALIDOMIDE

31 August 2017

It was a stark image I will never forget. An attractive, white-haired woman, who was much younger than she looked and obviously in discomfort, leaning on a crutch in a meeting room at a Sheraton hotel in Perth. Across the room, past a woman in a wheelchair, another middle-aged woman leaned against the wall.

Standing, not because there weren't enough seats for the fifty people crowded into a committee room, but because they were in too much pain to sit.

Welcome to the nightmarish world of thousands of Australian women who, over the past decade, had polypropylene mesh implanted in their bodies—sometimes without their knowledge. Many times done after surgeons had downplayed or glossed over the risks of crippling side effects.

And welcome to another public hearing of a Senate committee I fought to establish last year: a Perth hearing of the Senate Community Affairs References Committee into 'the number of women in Australia who had had trans-vaginal mesh implants and related matters'.

The woman leaning on the crutch was Stella Channing. I don't know how old she is but she has a young, impressively attentive daughter named Michaela, who hovered over her mother during the eight-hour public (and sometimes private) recounting of horror stories last week.

I now know that before being fitted with the controversial mesh, Stella was a physical fitness instructor. She said that after persevering all day at the hearing, she'll 'be in bed for a week'.

I won't pre-empt the Senate committee here. We have more public hearings in Sydney and Canberra next month.

Our Perth visit was only happening because I was approached by Caz Chisholm, a victim, and the founder of the Australian Pelvic Mesh Support Group. She emailed me from Perth, complaining that GPs, surgeons and politicians (state and federal) had ignored mesh victims for years.

The life raft group Caz and Stella are involved with started in 2014. At the beginning of 2017 they had 300 members. They now have more than 1200.

When I agreed to meet her, Caz Chisholm took the red-eye from Perth to Melbourne that night. And a South Australian victim, Kim Blieschke, drove from Port Pirie to Adelaide and then flew on to Melbourne.

It wasn't until I met other victims, who perched gingerly on a chair's edge and declined a taxi because they 'preferred to stand up in the train', that I realised how painful car and plane travel was for thousands of afflicted Australian women.

Some of them retold their graphic and painful stories in Melbourne. And I want to thank all these brave women whose intimate experiences should only have been shared behind closed doors with their doctors—if only their doctors had listened to and believed them.

A federal election is due when? The rhetoric and hyperbole of this week—as we prepare for another bruising Canberra session next week—could have convinced you a poll was merely weeks away.

What language! From the government frontbenchers came warnings of a Shorten government producing *1984*-style socialist economies. 'East German' in style, said Mathias Cormann. Like 'Cuba', said the Manchurian candidate, Josh Frydenberg.

On the other side we had Bill Shorten calling the prime minister 'weak'. I think the word 'coward' even snuck in there somewhere.

It's all still far short of the Master Paul Keating's jibes that 'a soufflé never rises twice' (Andrew Peacock), 'All tip, no iceberg' (Costello), or likening the Libs to 'a dog return[ing] to his vomit'.

Not quite that graphic yet, but a federal election is still two years away.

———

As the 'Yes' or 'No' debate over marriage equality intensifies, at least John Howard has come clean about the reason for the 2004 changes to the *Marriage Act*—which Labor supported. And that, when in office, Labor did not attempt to change, despite having an atheist and progressive PM in Julia Gillard. And which did not go to a plebiscite.

Former prime minister Howard admitted recently that the main reason for the explicit man/woman tightening of the Act was that the government did not want couples in same-sex relationships who married overseas to use the courts to set a precedent that could legalise same-sex marriage in Australia.

> What we didn't want to happen in 2004 was for the courts to start adjudicating on the definition of marriage because that was a real threat in 2004 because some people who had contracted same-sex marriages in another country had the capacity to bring their issues before courts in Australia. There was no definition in the *Marriage Act* in 2004 for the simple reason it had never occurred to the people before 2004 that marriage was other than between a man and a woman.

It has occurred to hundreds of millions of people around the world since then.

I'M NOT A GODDAM YANK

7 September 2017

Over the weekend, I was at that venerable Sydney watering hole, the Lord Nelson, at The Rocks, for a reunion, twenty years on, of people who worked in the newsroom and on the Hinch and Clive Robertson programs at John Singleton's 2GB.

I was also celebrating the fact that, over the same weekend, it was decreed in Canberra that I really am an Aussie, not a Kiwi, and certainly not whistling Dixie as a pseudo-Yank.

As I tweeted: *Attorney-General Brandis says Govt has cleared my S44 legitimacy. Won't refer to High Court. Opposition Leader Penny Wong agrees. Huge relief.*

It *was* a massive relief, especially when I had diligent, devoted staff wondering if they'd still have a job.

I will confess, I could see the lighter side. At the radio reunion, I sidled up to Mike Jeffreys (2UE–2GB, now Sky), Jason Morrison (2GB–2UE now Channel Seven Sydney news director) and my radio producer, Nicky Clement Elliott (now an award-winning documentary maker). I offered to buy them the first round and produced an American greenback $100 note.

Gotta laugh as this citizenship schmozzle gets crazier by the week. Or you'd go crazy.

Especially when, in the middle of the madness, Twitter trolls started claiming that my US social security number saga was a self-created publicity stunt.

And it got worse when Samantha Maiden and Ashleigh Gillon of Sky News and the Poison Dwarf—Steve Price, of 2GB and 3AW—joined in with the trolls and their 'stunt' theory.

Eventually, I published the accusatory email I'd received from the *Herald Sun*'s veteran reporter Keith Moor, which began:

> Dear Derryn, I have been contacted by somebody who claims you still have a current US social security card and/or green card and by doing so may be in breach of section 44 as a result of the fact holders of such cards are eligible for benefits from the US and section 44 states you can be disqualified from being a federal politician if you are entitled to the rights and privileges of a subject or a citizen of a foreign power.

On that dual citizenship issue I thought that Senator Katy Gallagher's explanation was one of the most eloquent and most convincing of them all—how her English mother was born in Ecuador but in the British embassy grounds, in a birth never registered in Ecuador. One Nation's Malcolm Roberts's was the least convincing.

And wasn't it great on Monday that opposition leader Bill Shorten finally produced his 'I'm not a Pom' paperwork in the House of Reps? Okay, it took him three damaging weeks—but it took Tony Abbott three years.

———

This is not a 17 per cent rush of blood to the head. But Malcolm Turnbull's increase in his lead over Bill Shorten as preferred prime minister may be a sign that the government's new, and belated, Kill Bill strategy may be working.

Maybe it is too late, but I am one of the few people in Canberra (I suspect on both sides) who thinks Bill and Chloe should not be picking out curtain material for the Lodge just yet.

I know senior cabinet ministers were angry, in retrospect (after their margin shrank to one seat), because they had listened to the 'experts' and shelved their 'Get Shorten' strategy in the marathon campaign last year.

They won't make that mistake again.

The shonky money deals, exposed by the royal commission, are already being flagged again by Michaelia Cash in the Senate. Keep watching for more.

———

Going back to the Lord Nelson, as I did at the weekend, it was my old stomping ground when living on Kent Street in Sydney in the mid 1990s.

On Sunday, in a quiet moment, I went back to the same corner table where I used to devour the papers over a dark ale while picking at a ploughman's lunch.

It brought back memories of another Sunday, a couple of decades ago, when I sat in that corner wading through the papers and the cheese and pickled onions.

I got a phone tip from a contact in Tasmania that 'something big's going on in Hobart'. He said, 'Maybe three or four people dead.' Half an hour later an update: 'Hinchy. I'm hearing there could be ten dead.'

As a new 'star' at 2GB I had some clout. I'd only been on air there for about a month. I raced into the station, threw the footy off air and broadcast live for the next five hours. It was the Port Arthur massacre.

I then grabbed a flight to Melbourne, another one to Launceston, and drove through the night to Hobart to talk to survivors.

A funny footnote. John Singleton, who had hired me for the morning shift on 2GB against his mate John Laws, was driving back from the Blue Mountains in the Roller that Sunday afternoon and decided to tune into his radio station to listen to the football.

He heard my voice and made a mental note: 'Must call the bloody station and tell them that Hinch promo is too fucking long.'

Then it dawned on him that it wasn't a station promo. Something really big was going on.

CHUCK AND DI AND THE PALACE PAPERS

14 September 2017

With all the nostalgic media hoopla surrounding the twentieth anniversary of the death of Princess Di, you could be forgiven for assuming that the 'Palace letters' had something do with her or Chuck or Camilla. Maybe an acerbic exchange between Prince Philip and the Princess of Wales, telling her to pull her pretty head in.

Nothing could be further from the truth. The mysterious contents of the Palace letters featured in an Australian courtroom last week, but the momentous occasion was almost media-free because of the focus on the High Court and the unsuccessful attempts to block the Turnbull government's same-sex marriage postal survey.

'Morse the pity' (as Jacki Weaver would say) because these letters could be the missing piece in the jigsaw that was the biggest political event in Australian history—the dismissal of the Whitlam government by the tippler in the top hat, Sir John Kerr.

The letters are the personal exchanges between the governor-general and Whitehall in the weeks (maybe months) leading up to the Dismissal. They reportedly air Sir Jonkers's understandable fears that, if Gough got wind of what his turncoat was plotting, it would be Kerr being shown the door, not Whitlam.

The correspondence was being fought over in Federal Court because university professor and Whitlam biographer Jenny Hocking has been fighting for their public release for years.

Commonwealth records are open after thirty years—which would have made them public in 2005—but the Palace letters have been designated 'personal' records and, on the instructions of the British, they are embargoed until at least 2027, with the sovereign's private secretary even retaining a veto after that.

The letters were between the governor-general and the Queen, her private secretary, Sir Michael Charteris, and Prince Charles, in the weeks before the Dismissal. Ironically, they are held by the National Archives in Canberra—not for access by us, but, it seems, for protection from us.

According to Hocking, Kerr's own records show that he confided in Prince Charles in September 1975 (a month before supply was blocked in the Senate) that he was considering dismissing Whitlam and was worried about his own position. Charles passed that on to Charteris and told Kerr, 'But surely Sir John, the Queen should not have to accept advice that you should be recalled … should this happen when you were considering having to dismiss the government.'

According to Kerr's records, Charteris then wrote to Kerr in early October, reassuring him that if 'the contingency to which you refer' should arise and if Whitlam moved to recall him as governor-general, then the palace would 'delay things'.

All this shows why these so-called 'personal letters', involving the most tumultuous time in Australian government, should be released. Will Turnbull ever urge the Queen to release the Whitlam Dismissal letters?

Fittingly, the QC arguing the case for their publication was Antony Whitlam QC—son of Gough.

————————

While we're on flashbacks, more than thirty years ago, in September 1985, the Hawke cabinet decided, and treasurer Paul Keating announced, we would have the Australia Card.

Having long held an American social security card (the one that caused me so much dual citizenship strife last week) I wasn't spooked and told then-health minister Neal Blewett, on 3AW, he could sign me up as 000 000 000 1.

It didn't happen. Civil libertarians went apeshit and the Australia Card was abandoned in 1986, although some aspects of it survived in 1988 in the tax file number legislation.

I called a fellow senator a 'boofhead' on Twitter the other day. Some might call that unparliamentary language, but I would argue that truth is a defence in some states.

The tweet said: *Senator 'Boofhead' Burston now claims I'm a UK dual citizen. As I told the Oz: 'Christ, I was an American last week, now I'm a Pom.' Not true.*

In a rambling, disjointed adjournment speech that Burston said 'might be a bit cryptic for some to understand', he obliquely urged me to resign:

> The honourable thing to do would be to jump before being pushed. The noose will be tightening around this person's neck soon, and perhaps their head will be small enough to put on a slouch hat. Perhaps their next job will be selling chocolates for charity on *The Footy Show*.

Even though I used to have a business connection with Slouch Hat Chocolates and the RSL, I didn't think this rancid rant was aimed at me, because I've never claimed to hold UK citizenship and Boofhead had said earlier:

… there's been one person at least who has attempted to manipulate the situation to be more about putting the spotlight on themselves than on resolving this debacle. In the public domain, they have claimed to be a UK citizen by descent, but they were born elsewhere—not Australia nor the UK. Have they renounced their UK citizenship or was their original claim just a lie? If we were to take their statements prior to them entering parliament at face value, they wouldn't have a passport and wouldn't be here—or were those statements lies too?

A Burston staffer confirmed to media that 'Hinch was the target … we're gunning for him.'

It seems the senator had read in one of my books (apparently, he does read) that my grandparents were English. I just hope he bought it and didn't get it out of the library.

GHOSTS FROM THE PAST

21 September 2017

What a feast for an investigative journo, after the speaker of the House of Reps, Tony Smith, and the Senate president, Stephen Parry, agreed, surprisingly, to release the suppressed details of an inquiry into the murky work of former Whitlam government attorney-general, and controversial High Court judge, Lionel Murphy. An inquiry shut down, and details sealed, when Murphy got terminal cancer.

As his cesspool hometown local paper, the *Daily Telegraph*, headlined it this week: 'Sin City'.

It did have everything, starting with that famous (infamous) Murphy quote to a magistrate about immigration

solicitor Morgan Ryan: 'Now, what about my little mate?'
And it went on to implicate the real 'Mr Sin', Abe Saffron, the
pre-Ibrahim lord of Kings Cross, plus crooked magistrates, and
Murphy's (alleged) intervention with premier Neville 'Nifty
Nev' Wran to get the new long-term Luna Park contract
flick-passed to Abe.

(Remember that ghost train fire that killed all those kids
before the transfer? Was that possibly arson?)

There were further allegations that Murphy conspired
with Saffron to have a witness roughed up and that he not
only sampled the offerings at one of Mr Sin's brothels, he part-
owned it.

All of this, when I was actually in the NSW parliament
building for another gruelling week of Senate committee
public hearings into the transvaginal mesh scandal. We talked
to some Scottish mesh survivors. I said, last year in the Senate
speech that triggered our public inquiry, that it was 'the worst
medical scandal for Australian women since Thalidomide'.

The Scottish witnesses said they had the backing of
Thalidomide supporters, who said this scandal, internationally,
was even worse. There was one new expression I heard this
week I wish I hadn't had to hear: a crippled mesh victim talked
about 'forever pain'. Day and night, 24/7. Diabolical.

———————

Anyway, I won't concentrate on Lionel, or transvaginal mesh,
because, as I started writing this, I saw a promo on Sky News
for 'Jones & Co'. Alan Jones and Peta Credlin were going
to interview former prime minister Tony Abbott. Hold the
front page.

First, we had to plough through the corn. Jones: 'Welcome
to the Peta Alan show.' The pair discussed their matching
(Liberal) blue ensembles. And then Alan Jones went into a

TV editorial rant that must have lasted fifteen minutes. On television, not radio. I did tweet in frustration: *Sky invents radio on TV. Fifteen minutes of Alan Jones's ranting head on prime time. No overlay, no background pics. Just a full-on rant.*

The Credlin–Abbott show was incredible. Niki Savva would have been scribbling furiously. At times, Peta looked like a leonine, dark-haired Nicole Kidman on a facially enhanced expressionless day. Amazing muscle control. She did interrupt her former boss to say 'correct me if I'm wrong'. He didn't. And he didn't slip and call her 'Chief'.

Throughout it, we had to suffer Jones's saccharine simpering. Like when he said, 'You should be running the show,' and 'We can't win the election with Turnbull as leader,' and, I'm sure, in the next breath, he then endorsed Peta for PM. Vomitsville.

———

I did preserve for posterity one Alan Jones quote from the Abbott lovefest. The breakfast serial spruiker did say, on the record, to Peta Credlin, 'You're a farming lady and so am I.'

———

Speaking of Lionel Murphy prompts the memory of one of those 'what if' moments that could change the path of history.

Not many people know this, but, Lionel Murphy gave the phone number of Canberra femme fatale Junie Morosi to Andrew Peacock—before Jim Cairns got hold of it, bedded her and hired her. Years later, Peacock told me that, late one night, he'd looked at the phone number on a crumpled piece of paper, and decided not to dial it.

Reminded me of a possibly apocryphal 'what if' story about when President Nixon first met Chairman Mao. Behind the Bamboo Curtain, as we used to call China's isolation, Nixon himself was burbling on with a 'what if' story about the slain President Kennedy: what would have happened to the world if it had been the Soviet leader, Nikita Khrushchev, who was assassinated in November 1963 and not JFK?

Mao supposedly ruminated and then sagely opined, 'I'm sure of one thing. Aristotle Onassis would not have married Mrs Khrushchev.'

That queen of the punsters, Kathy Lette, this week tweeted a wonderful indictment of the scourge known as text messaging.

She reported, straight-faced or straight-keyboard, that the inventor of predictive text had left this world. As Kathy put it, he had 'pissed away and his funfair will be held next monkey'.

THEY ACTUALLY DO WORK HARD

28 September 2017

This is a genuine personal political mea culpa. Last year, as the 45th federal parliament wound down for the Christmas–New Year break, they released the sitting schedule for the Senate for 2017.

Senator 'Wet behind the ears' Hinch took to the floor, in that rarified world of red leather, and castigated his colleagues for agreeing to sit for 'only' fifteen weeks.

Haven't checked Hansard, but I'm sure I thundered it was 'a disgrace'.

Attorney-general George Brandis made the droll observation, 'Wait until you've been here a few months.'

George was right, in spades. To the extent that, when I walk into my Melbourne apartment building, when the Senate is not sitting, I bristle when a lift-sharer cheerfully says, 'Enjoying your holiday?'

I know this sounds like a politician being a politician, but this brand-new world of mine has proven to be a lot more work than I thought.

In addition to sitting weeks, there are marathon weeks (9 a.m.–11 p.m. days) of estimates committee hearings where ministers and public servants get grilled about money matters—and anything else that gets under the bonnet of people like senator Doug Cameron.

Plus: all senators on review committees have daunting schedules for public hearings around the country.

In my case, I have held hearings in Sydney, Melbourne, Perth and Canberra about the crippling after-effects of the implantation of transvaginal mesh into thousands of unsuspecting, ill-informed Australian women.

Anyway, enough of the job justification. I already can hear the Twitterverse: *Quit ya bitchin', Hinch. That's what we pay you heaps for.*

———————

Blow the siren. To use a grand final week analogy, we're still only in the first quarter of the $122 million marriage equality postal survey/ballot/non-plebiscite/opinion poll but already people are sick of it—bored with it leading the news bulletins and talkback programs daily.

(On Sky News, where they pass the same-sex marriage baton from program to program, Paul Murray has the right idea. In his two-hour nightly show, he has a 'same-sex marriage survey minute'.)

Fervent supporters of marriage equality have already cast their 'Yes' votes but what if, in the seemingly interminable weeks ahead, apathy starts to eat into people's good intentions and the participation rate drops below 50 per cent? What sort of mandate is that for either side?

It reminds me of a line my mother used to say: 'I took my harp to a party—and nobody asked me to play.'

———————

I foolishly engaged Vote No campaigner senator Cory Bernardi on Twitter after he accused me of headline-hunting. It came as my Twitter feed descended into cruel, intolerant, inaccurate crap from both sides of the gay marriage 'debate'.

It prompted this tweeted promise: *SSM. Was wrong to take Bernardi bait. Won't again. In fact: want to clear my Twitter page of SSM. I shan't post or respond. May delete.*

Self-censorship is hard, but I've stuck to it. I'll confess I have cheated a couple of times by retweeting some arguments I've agreed with. Or 'with which I have agreed', as Churchill would have said.

———————

Running parallel to the 'What constitutes marriage?' debate— with the 'No' advocates insisting it has been between a man and a woman at least 'for a millennium'—has been the cultural issue of child brides.

It has been in the headlines recently because of a rare prosecution in Victoria, where a Muslim man has been jailed, and an imam given a suspended sentence, after a 'marriage' involving a 14-year-old girl.

It's encouraging to see columnists now calling it what it really is: child rape. That's what this man was originally charged with, but the director of public prosecutions permitted the charge to be plea-bargained down.

And the mother should have been charged with aiding and abetting after she sold her daughter for a $1500 gold trinket.

One startling historical fact this issue has flushed out is how recently some Australian states permitted men to take child brides. Girls even younger than fourteen, and I presume with the parents' permission.

According to Fairfax columnist Peter Hartcher, quoting Macquarie University professor Shirleene Robinson, the minimum legal age for females to marry in Tasmania was twelve—until it was raised to sixteen in 1942.

And a 12-year-old girl could still legally get married in Western Australia until 1956. Learn something every day.

I mentioned time-consuming Senate committees earlier. I am on a working committee trying to streamline chamber times and business. Trying to give more speakers more opportunities. Especially crossbenchers.

What the major parties have failed to realise, or chosen to ignore, is that the Senate makeup has changed. Forever. The crossbench is a disparate, sometimes desperate, political reality. The Greens, Xenophon, PHON and the rest of us make up more than a quarter of the seventy-six senators. And we ain't going away. At the next federal election, the non-government or ALP Senate vote could top 30 per cent.

The all-party committee is looking at cutting twenty-minute speeches to fifteen (in line with the House of Reps) and reducing some adjournment speeches to five and ten-minuters only.

Again, my personal campaign is to also scrap supplementary questions in question time. Especially the government backbenchers' Dorothy Dixers.

I cringe when a minister gushes: 'I thank the member for Macquariesquat for that incisive question.' It was a question written in the minister's office. And the stumbling way the member reads it, we are all well aware that's the first time they've seen it. And they're only on their feet because it's their turn. Scrap it and send out a media release.

SOPHIE YORK, PLEASE STOP EMAILING ME. I ALREADY VOTED YES.

5 October 2017

Time again to invoke the name of that crazy, wild-haired professor, Julius Sumner Miller. As he used to intone on the telly, 'Why is it so?'

I want to apply it to the $122 million 'secret' postal survey being conducted for the federal government (with the imprimatur of the High Court) to see if Australians like the idea of people of the same sex being permitted to legally marry—as is now the case in more than twenty other countries.

I have put the word 'secret' in quotes even though last week I spent two hours being lectured about ballot secrecy by staff from the Australian Bureau of Statistics at the massive Fuji Xerox data-management and mail-sorting plant at an industrial complex in Moorebank near Liverpool, in Sydney.

We were told how even though Fuji got the bar-coded ballot papers, they were never linked to the electoral roll and the same applied in reverse to the ABS. The only way anybody could know how somebody voted was if they had scrawled their name on the form. And, anyway, the observers sign confidentiality agreements.

Under escort, I visited the initial processing room for the millions of envelopes. It was like something out of a Kubrick movie: about forty people were sitting at desks, wearing protective gowns, goggles and breathing masks. All precautions, in case somebody added powder (or worse) to their contribution to democracy.

One group slit open the envelopes. Others extracted and smoothed the forms—for electronic or manual counting—and separated any extraneous material. All under the eyes of security guards. Tedious but important work.

Cue Sumner Miller: 'Why is it so?' Or, how come this is so, if the ballot is so secret?

A dear friend, Lynda Stoner, posted her ballot paper on a recent Sunday, and the following Friday received an email from Sarah Midgley at Vote Yes for Equality, thanking her for her 'Yes' vote.

The email from allofus@equalitycampaign.org.au said:

Lynda—

Thank you so much for posting your YES vote! You and so many other Australians are helping to achieve marriage equality. This campaign has momentum—we're getting a really positive response all across the country.

We can't rest on our laurels though. If we're going to win we need to turn every YES supporter into a YES voter. It's now about making sure our friends and family have posted their YES votes.

There are still millions of survey forms waiting to be returned. That's why we've created a new tool to help you encourage your friends to post their YES votes. Click here to email 5 friends and remind them to post their YES votes. We know that people are far more likely to post their votes if a friend or family member reminds them. That's why it's far more effective if you email—we've just made it easy.

Now, Stoner is CEO of Animal Liberation in Sydney and the email went to lynda@animal-lib.org.au. She has been a passionate supporter of just causes for decades and did vote yes on this one.

But how did the Yes campaign know that she had just voted and how she had voted? Julius, I'm keen to know.

Maybe it comes under the category 'assumptive junk mail'.

———————

And now let's hear from the other side. Apart from my senatorial dot com email address, I have a 'Hillary Clinton account' at hinch@hinch.net.

I get mail there addressed to 'hinch' and 'Darren' and 'Bleepwit' and some youngsters even send mail to 'Dezza'. But, after a year as 'Senator Hinch', I resent getting emails addressed to 'Dear Media Deryn' or 'Media Dery'.

Sophie York, the spokeswoman for Marriage Alliance, has been bombarding me. (And isn't 'Marriage Alliance' such a non-threatening, non-confronting name? Alliance with whom?)

She's told me about inspiring speeches from senator Cory Bernardi and about the mystery benefactor who has offered $200 000 and asked if people like me would donate towards a matching $200 000.

And hammering the red herring that 'the implications of a "yes" vote on freedom of speech and belief would be huge, and all Australians will be affected!' Doesn't seem to be affecting hers or Cory's or Tony Abbott's.

Haven't had the heart to email back and tell Sophie I've already voted yes, that I'm on the Senate Yes vote observation team and have done a personal cover version of Kermit singing 'The Rainbow Connection' on the Justice Party's Facebook page.

———————

The Las Vegas massacre brought back awful memories of Port Arthur. I flew into Hobart only a few hours after that slaughter. To my surprise, the roulette tables and the pokies were all in full swing at Wrest Point Casino. I snapped at some revellers in the hotel lobby when they asked, 'Hey, Hinchy, you here on holidays?'

In the lift, I met a man who said quietly, 'They got my Gwen.' His name was Ron Neander. His wife, Gwen, was killed by Martin Bryant in the Broad Arrow Cafe, that April Sunday back in 1996.

IT IS A TRAGEDY THAT NICK XENOPHON IS LEAVING THE SENATE

12 Ocotber 2017

If I were a voter in South Australia right now, I would be mightily pissed off. About eighteen months ago, Malcolm Turnbull inflicted one of the longest federal election campaigns ever on this country with a double dissolution. Voters in all states were compelled to go to the polls and elect (or re-elect) twelve senators as well as members of the House of Reps. I loved it. Got me elected.

Two of the senators elected in South Australia were that true-blue Liberal Cory Bernardi and maverick Nick Xenophon. Both elected for six years.

Within months of being re-elected, Bernardi scored a cushy sinecure (at taxpayers' expense) with a secondment to the United Nations, where he seemed to spend much of his time hanging out with Donald Trump supporters.

When he got back, he announced that the Liberal Party was too liberal for him and he jumped ship to sit on the crossbench as founder of (and sole senator from) the Australian Conservatives.

Bernardi didn't resign his Senate seat and let the Libs appoint another senator. He just took their seat and 're-badged it' (to use a Xenophon term).

And, speaking of Nick, he won a six-year term on 2 July last year. South Australians voted for the NXT (the Nick Xenophon Team) but they were really voting for Nick personally, and the other two SA senators coat-tailed him. The same way a lot of Australians voted for Pauline Hanson and her coat-tails pulled in Rod Culleton (now gone from WA), and Brian 'Boofhead' Burston in NSW, and Malcolm (soon to be gone) Roberts—Mr seventy-seven votes—in Queensland.

Now, less than eighteen months later, Xenophon announces he's going home. He's quitting the Senate to go play in the South Australian state election next year, as a small-pond powerbroker/kingmaker/self-promoter.

What about the other four-and-a-half years he was committed to serve as party leader and voters' rep, as a crossbench wheeler and dealer in the Senate?

Forgeddit, as the Americans would say. But Nick, whom I will be sorry to see leave the red benches, has form on this.

His first political coup was to finagle enough preference deals to get his anti-pokies platform an upper house seat in Adelaide. That was supposedly for eight years but, within two, Nick X announced that stage was too small and too insignificant for him.

Now he's giving his Senate supporters the bird.

At least if somebody leaves 'the other place' in a hurry (as deputy PM and National Party leader Barnaby Joyce may soon have to do), the voters get to have their say at a by-election.

In the Senate, there is no such opportunity. Shortly after Cory Bernardi betrayed his party, and his voters, he rose in his seat to talk about principles.

It was so hypocritical, I had to join in:

> To hear him stand there talking about principle, after he stood as a Liberal candidate and was elected by the people of South Australia as a Liberal candidate, is a joke.
>
> I want to go on record to say that I find it appalling that this has happened.

I pointed out that if somebody in the lower house changes their philosophy or opinions, and does not like their party's principles anymore, they should resign their seat. (Are you listening, Mr Abbott?)

They can then go back to the people at the resulting by-election and say, 'This is who I am, this is what I stand for now,' and test their standing.

Unfortunately, in the Senate that doesn't apply, which I personally don't believe is the most democratic way to do things.

And to finish up back on South Australia: I haven't even mentioned Lucy Gichuhi, who was a Family First after-thought, following Bob Day's expulsion, and who decided to take the Senate seat as an independent when her FF Party nabobs decided to throw in their lot with Bernardi's Conservatives.

I mentioned Malcolm's marathon election campaign— which took him within one seat of losing the keys to the Lodge. The fledgling Justice Party started campaigning four months before the PM called that election. Covered 11 250 kilometres in the Justice Bus in Victoria and country NSW.

I promised that, if elected, I would go back to rural and regional centres every month. Not just after an election had been called.

We have been to many, including Wangaratta, Shepparton, Beechworth, Inverloch and Melton. This week, by train and car, our team has been to Bendigo, Swan Hill and Mildura. I have talked to local police chiefs, mayors and councillors. Every night we have honoured The Ode of Remembrance at the local RSL.

I have a word of warning for the Turnbull team. Your guys scoffed last year when I reported back that disgruntled 'rusted-on' Liberal voters were scared and angry about changes to superannuation.

This year (and leading up to the federal election) it's power prices. Nobody wants to talk about anything else. Domestic electricity bills are sapping families. And business too. I even got bailed up last week by a man with a medium-sized business in McMahons Point, on Sydney's north shore, who said his power bill is now $700 000 a year. You can't cover that by just increasing your own product prices.

Travel note: was surprised, and encouraged, by the number of new vineyards springing up from Bendigo to Mildura. Happy to report that a glass of shiraz from Heathcote can compete with any wine in the world. Trentham's pretty good too.

THE UNSEEMLY MESSAGE TONY ABBOTT LEFT ON MY VOICEMAIL

19 October 2017

It's not every day a former PM gives you such gratuitous advice.

Hey, I didn't make the call. Tony Abbott did.

That was my reaction when the Twitter trolls came after me in a torrent following my revelation on *Paul Murray Live* on Sky News that the former prime minister had given me some gratuitous advice: 'Shut the fuck up.'

Some of the twitterati claimed I must have made it up because 'Mr Abbott would never use that sort of language'. Some thought it was 'fake news', as the Donald would say. And I will concede it's the sort of unseemly, and potentially damaging, message I would never leave on anybody's telephone message bank. Friend or foe.

But an angry Tony Abbott did.

I said, on Paul Murray's eponymous show, that it was a few weeks ago. I have since checked back and worked out that the abusive message was left on Thursday, June 22. (I now recall the timetable because that was the week they had the dry-run anti-terrorist security lockdown of Parliament House.)

I had been on Sky the night before and repeated something I'd said on Neil Mitchell's 3AW program the day before: that some Abbott supporters were so relentlessly determined to destroy Malcolm Turnbull they were leaking to Bill Shorten's office. I'd heard News Corp was also onto the story.

An irate Tony Abbott got my super-private phone number from a mutual friend, introduced himself, and left a message demanding that I provide him with proof to back up what I had said, or name the source for what I'd said. 'Otherwise,' he said, 'shut the fuck up.'

I played it to my staff in Melbourne that morning and also in a 'guess who?' quiz with my former *Hinch* producer Dermot O'Brien, at our regular Romeo's lunch catch-up in Toorak two days after it happened.

It came up again last week only because Abbott had made headlines with his goats and volcanoes 'climate change does more good than harm' speech in London. Then another former prime minister, Julia Gillard, gave the 2017 Bob Hawke lecture in Adelaide and started talking about the election of Donald Trump as President and Brexit and an 'age of anxiety'.

I was asked about former prime ministers airing their views and suggested Tony Abbott, upon whom we bestowed the 'Mad Monk' moniker, should, perhaps, heed his own message-machine advice.

And now, in reference to the NEG—the National Energy Guarantee—let's talk about chewing gum.

Winston Peters, currently playing kingmaker across the ditch, almost cost the Labour government the 2005 election when he derisively shot down finance minister Michael Cullen's budget 'chewing gum' tax cuts.

They were such a big deal, and so generous to the worker, the New Zealand First leader said, that everybody would be able to afford a pack of chewing gum.

If the Turnbull/Frydenberg NEG predictions are accurate, in 2020 your electricity bill will have come down by $2 a week. Bring on the chewing gum!

To be fair, I don't believe NEG is an abbreviation of negativity (as the Greens and Labor would have you believe). And I don't believe it is a Turnbull kowtow to Abbott. I also don't believe it signals an exit from the Paris Agreement that (pre goats and volcanoes) the Abbott government signed. Give it a chance.

———————

Speaking of chances. It is hard to believe that it will be ten years next month since prime minister John Howard not only lost office but also lost his own seat—the first PM to achieve (?) that distinction since Stanley Bruce in 1929.

It was an ignominious end for a politician who, before he regained his party's leadership and then the keys to the Lodge, had said he would have to be 'Lazarus with a triple bypass' to make a comeback.

You have to wonder if yon Lazarus ever creeps into Tony Abbott's thoughts these days.

He was asked on 2GB this week about comebacks and said, 'When you're an ex [leader] the only way you can come back is if you are drafted. That's a pretty rare and unusual business in politics. The only way an ex could ever come back is by way of a draft and that's almost impossible to imagine.'

But you can dream.

––––––––––––

During last year's federal election campaign, we covered 11 250 kilometres in the Justice Bus and I promised, if elected, I'd keep going back to rural and regional Victoria. At least once a month.

Last week's adventure by train and car was to Bendigo, Swan Hill and Mildura. In each town, we visited the local RSL club just in time for the 6 p.m. recital of The Ode '… at the going down of the sun …' It's a great, stirring, tradition.

In Mildura, I caught up with the old and the new in the veterans' world: 92-year-old former Nationals MP Ken Wright and Afghanistan war veteran, Tyson Matheson.

FRAUDS MAKE KILLING OUT OF DUGONG MEAT

26 October 2017

Endangered animals continue to be hunted unsustainably with the immunity brought by Native Title.

I just don't get it. Colin Riddell, please explain. Actually, he is one of the few people in this country who doesn't have to. I mention his name because Riddell is a passionate conservationist who has been trying, for nearly a decade, to save threatened dugongs and sea turtles in Queensland. Endangered critters being slaughtered under the real farce of Native Title.

I say I don't get it, because—despite Senate speeches, recent visits to a turtle veterinary hospital in Cairns, and more questions this week in Senate estimates—I can't get any traction with the Liberals or with Labor. Or, shamefully, with the Greens. It has to be because they fear Indigenous antipathy.

It's one issue on which the Nats' Nigel Scullion and I part company, and environment minister Josh Frydenberg seems to be singing permanently from another song sheet these days. As did his predecessor Greg Hunt. Despite promises.

There are polystyrene eskies coming into the baggage carousel at Cairns Airport from the Torres Strait Islands. The eskies contain meat. It is turtle and dugong—not chicken. The turtle, I understand, is being sold for up to $80 a kilo, and the dugong for $130 a kilo. And this is happening in Cairns as we speak.

I've been involved in this campaign on radio and television for about eight years and have spent time with Riddell and Steve Irwin's father, Bob.

They have been promised the world and have been given dust.

At Senate estimates this week, I asked: 'I would like to know, under Native Title, how many dugongs and sea turtles are slaughtered every year in Queensland?' These are endangered creatures. They could be extinct in thirty years.

It was a legit question. As I said, 'I was on Green Island a couple of weeks ago. As the boat arrives they say this is a protected marine park and they warn you not even to pick up a piece of coral off the beach because it is a protected marine park. Yet, we have boats with outboard motors on them getting in amongst the swimmers on Green Island and slaughtering turtles with machetes, which surely was not the plan of the cultural system under Native Title?

'It is not cultural. It is not done with a spear. It is done with a modern boat with outboard motor and machete, chasing these beautiful creatures until they are exhausted and then they are killed.'

In Cairns, I talked to Aboriginal elders from the coastal clans, the coastal tribes, who have banned the killing of dugongs up there, but the rainforest tribes come down and the young bucks go out there in their motor boats and kill them. At the turtle veterinarian hospital, they tag them, take them 50 kilometres out to sea and they are still tracked and killed within twenty-four hours. Surely that is not what Native Title was designed to do for cultural reasons?

———————

I am thick. Just didn't get it. In the midst of Malcolm Turnbull and Josh Frydenberg talking up the NEG and the apparent solving of the domestic power price crisis, I didn't get the hidden Freudian message.

NEG—the National Energy Guarantee. The cartoonists, like me, zeroed in on the negative aspects of the NEG.

It took my brother, Des, visiting from across the ditch, and an aficionado of Australian politics, to point out what should have been obvious.

'They're talking endlessly about the NEG policy, the N-E-G policy, solving the energy crisis. Energy, don't you get it?'

I do now.

———————

At 2.15 p.m. tomorrow the High Court will hand down its dual citizenship verdict on the Munificent Seven. I'll be on a plane back from Melbourne from the Daniel Morcombe memorial red T-shirt walk in Maroochydore, in Queensland. I will ask the pilot to relay the message.

Hinch's Hunch (and I'm often wrong) is that the safest of the Seven is Nick Xenophon. Roberts is well gone. And the Greens, Ludlam and Walters, resigned anyway.

———————

I know this is 'off the west wall', as they used to say in newsagency talk, but I'm getting really sick of mispronunciations, or should that be 'mis-pronounciations'? And some of our pollies are the worst offenders.

It's Los 'Angelis', not Los 'Angeleese'. It's 'Los' Vegas, not 'Lass' Vegas. Nuclear is 'nuclee-a', not 'nuke-u-lah'. And it's not a bloody medium strip either!

I call prostate cancer the 'lying down disease' because so many people call it 'prostrate' cancer.

And, on planes, listen to the safety instructions and wait for a mention of the emergency 'egg-sit'. The letter 'x' has been replaced by a 'g'.

FORMER UNDERTAKER STEPHEN PARRY CARRIED OUT IN CITIZENSHIP BOX

2 November 2017

I fly a lot. Got so friendly with a TWA flight attendant on a White House press charter that I married her. Once, arriving for a flight across Fiji from Nadi to Suva, I was told they had overbooked. They asked if I'd fly in the co-pilot's seat. For the whole trip over the mountains I studied the pilot for signs of a pending heart attack.

On a flight from Cairns to Sydney after that infamous Ansett bomb scare cover-up—which I revealed on *Hinch*—the pilot sent a note back with the hostie. It said: 'If I'd known you were on my flight, I would have had you thrown off in Brisbane.'

So, I was a bit wary last Friday, asking a Virgin cockpit crew for a favour. You see, as the EST clock ticked towards 2.15 p.m., I was on a flight from Maroochydore to Melbourne after the Day for Daniel walk. Totally shut off from the High Court ruling on the political futures of the Munificent Seven. Could the cockpit crew get info from the ground and pass it on?

I knew, 'in my gut', we were right when we argued the deputy prime minister, Baa-naby Joyce, should have 'done a Canavan', like his Senate National Party colleague, and gone to the backbench while awaiting the High Court decision. And so should Senator Fiona Nash.

Joyce's 'gut feeling' admission, after the High Court decision, made it even more of a scandal. The National Party leader said, 'In my gut I thought this is the way it is going to go.'

Jesus wept. Surely this cornpone knew that this is not the US of A. That under section 64 of our constitution a cabinet member must be a member of Parliament? And that cabinet decisions, and ministerial decisions, made by a tainted minister, could face future legal challenges?

Not to mention the possible court cases down the track launched by commercial entities who could argue their business had been financially damaged by a (now illegal) ministerial ruling.

How was Barnyard Barnaby's gut feeling when, in a burst of dumb arrogance and over-confidence, the PM expressed total confidence in his deputy by insisting in question time that Joyce was 'qualified to sit in the house and the High Court will so hold'?

But back to my flight. Tick, tick, tick. Quarter past two arrived and a charming flight attendant named Lynda told me she would have a cockpit message very soon. And, within ten minutes, I was handed a friendly hand-scrawled note from the pilot across a telex-style printout detailing the two who were in and the five who were out.

Confession time. And this may be a breach of CASA or FAA or Virgin flight laws. The journo in me couldn't help himself. You never get the ink out of the veins.

Well before Lynda brought me the news, I had surreptitiously taken my iPhone off aeroplane mode under the lunch serviette and glanced at my messages. My trusted EA, Annette Philpott, had fired four words into the ether: 'Saved Xenophon and Canavan.' The flight attendant had been so helpful; I couldn't tell her that I already knew.

If I had to bet on who was the safest senator under section 44 I would have wagered that the least likely person to be carried out in the dual citizenship box would be the Senate president, former undertaker, Stephen Parry.

He was one of the most impressive people I met in the 45th parliament. A procedural stickler, he knew the law, and, as a former policeman, he knew right from wrong. So, I find it inexplicable, and totally out of character, that Parry did not put his own hand up, when, from the president's chair, he handed up the paperwork sending Senator Fiona Nash to the High Court. His case of having a father born in the UK mirrored hers.

And the various permutations and implications of Barnaby Joyce's parental predicament had flooded the media for months.

In his shock email to us this week, Parry wrote that 'My father moved to Australia as a boy in 1951.' Not too much of a boy. He married Parry's mother nine years later. The year Parry was born in Tasmania.

The email also had a Malcolm Roberts touch: 'I have always regarded my late father as Australian'. Maybe, but surely he knew his dad was a Pom. Even though he mentioned his family's convict roots in his maiden speech.

Wasn't the issue ever raised in the Liberal party room as the government dominoes kept falling?

More questions: Why did Senator Parry wait until this week? Is this why he cancelled a parliamentary trip to India last Friday? Was he hoping for a High Court decision that cleared Nash and Joyce and left him under the radar?

There are now even more forceful demands for an audit of all MPs' credentials. As I tweeted: *Stephen Parry, another domino. Cross-bench all voted for independent audit of us all. Libs, Nats, Labor blocked us. Will bring it on again.*

FROM BULLSHIT
TO BURQAS

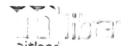

As I would have said, in my old comfortable, familiar world of television: 'TW3. That was the Year That Was.' And my first year as a senator in the 45th parliament of Australia was certainly one helluva year.

It started on the night of 2 July 2016, when opposition leader Bill Shorten made a speech that sounded like he had won.

And then Prime Minister Turnbull was shamed out of his sulking in a Sydney lair to make a spiteful late-night accusatory speech that reminded me of ex-PM Billy Snedden. He said, 'We were not beaten. We didn't win enough seats to form a government.'

Turnbull's strange performance was on par with Christopher Pyne's gloating comment about the Libs being an 'election-winning machine' when they had clung to office by just one seat.

I truly believe Bill Shorten would be in the Lodge right now if his Labor colleague Victorian premier Daniel Andrews had not been so shackled by his historic union connections that he could not extricate himself from a despicable union power play to neuter the Country Fire Authority. The awesome, and legendary, voluntary fire brigade.

During that marathon 2016 federal campaign, we started campaigning in the Justice Bus four months before Turnbull called the election. As I've said, we covered 11 250 kilometres in country Victoria and southern New South Wales. That's a lot of CFA sausage sizzles. The bully-boy state Labor government was on the nose, and I believe the reason Victoria was the only state where Labor lost ground (and actually lost a seat) was the CFA shit fight.

Anyway, let's move on. In this final chapter, I want to share some personal guidelines.

While compiling, and working on the nuts-and-bolts construction of this book, I wrote to Louise Adler, my publisher at MUP, and said:

> One thing I can't do, because it will affect the colour and flow of a diary, is to play 'Monday morning quarterback' and second-guess, or justify, or excuse what I wrote at the time. That would add another 40000 words to the book!

And that would have been true. It would have insulted you, the reader, were I to go back and dissect, excuse, justify, modify, what I had written on the day during a colourful, passionate time. The opinions expressed in these columns were those I held when it was all happening. They still, and must, stand alone.

So, let's look back at the 2016–17 season of the Australian parliament.

In the Senate, sadly, and I hate to acknowledge this, the most memorable moment of the year was Pauline Hanson's burqa stunt.

The work of her latest Svengali, James Ashby (formerly notorious for the sexual harassment case he unsuccessfully brought against one-time parliamentary speaker Peter Slipper), was all over it. Probably done at his instructions. He dressed Senator Hanson in the shroud, alerted security to get an escort to the chamber, and had a News Corp photographer in Hanson's office for the set-up.

So, what did it all look like from the Senate chamber side that day?

I sit right behind Pauline Hanson on the red leather benches. That afternoon her seat was empty. Not unusual. One Nation senators are rarely in the Senate chamber, even during question time. (Which is a disgrace and, I believe, a betrayal of constituents. We are paid to, at least, be there.)

That afternoon, from my vantage point at the back of the Senate, I saw One Nation NSW senator Brian 'Boofhead' Burston walk into the chamber from the other end, shepherding a woman shrouded in a burqa.

My honest initial assumption was that (unorthodox as it looked) he was guiding a guest through the chamber. It wasn't until Senate staff stepped in that I realised it was something else.

The black-clad anonymous woman then floated through the Senate, through growing verbal rumblings, and claimed Pauline Hanson's seat.

The Senate president, senator Stephen Parry, a former policeman and undertaker from Tasmania, assured the stunned, murmuring mass that the shrouded woman was, in fact, elected senator Pauline Hanson and immediately got on with question time.

I was shocked that the Senate would let this unsavoury stunt continue unchallenged. The president merely indicated that question time would continue as usual. Not one government or opposition member stood to protest what I believe/believed, was a calculated insult to our parliamentary system.

Finally, I managed to be heard by the president, on a point of order. I pointed out that, if it were in fact Pauline Hanson under that burqa (as he had assured the Senate), I had a question about Senate protocol.

I said we all knew that Senator Hanson, if that were indeed her under the shroud, was not a Muslim and not wearing a burqa for religious or cultural reasons, so did that mean I could now assume that I could wear fancy dress in the Senate the next sitting day?

I later extended this argument when talking to David Speers on Sky News, and on *Lateline* on the ABC. I made the point that, because of my well-known campaign against paedophiles, especially Catholic priests, could I now wear a cassock, and my collar turned back to front, next Senate sitting day? Or even wear a cardinal's costume?

When it was her turn to ask a question, the black-clad One Nation leader dramatically flung off her facial covering to ask the attorney-general (representing the prime minister) when would Australia ban the burqa?

Senator George Brandis said, off the cuff,

Senator Hanson, no, we will not be banning the burqa. Now, Senator Hanson, I am not going to pretend to ignore the stunt that you have tried to pull today by arriving in the chamber dressed in a burqa when we all know that you are not an adherent of the Islamic faith. I would caution you and counsel you, Senator Hanson, with respect, to be very, very careful of the offence you may do to the religious sensibilities of other Australians. We have about half a million Australians in this country of the Islamic faith, and the vast majority of them are law-abiding, good Australians. Senator Hanson, it is absolutely consistent being a good, law-abiding Australian and being a strict-adherent Muslim. Senator Hanson, for the last four years I have had responsibility, pre-eminently among the ministers, subject to the Prime Minister, for national security policy. And, I can tell you, Senator Hanson, that it has been the advice of each Director-General of Security with whom I have worked, and each Commissioner of the Australian Federal Police with whom I have worked, that it is vital for their intelligence and law enforcement work that they

work cooperatively with the Muslim community. To ridicule that community, to drive it into a corner, to mock its religious garments is an appalling thing to do, and I would ask you to reflect on what you have done.

To use the hackneyed phrase, the air was electric. Someone to my right on the Greens bench started to applaud and it was picked up by other crossbenchers (except One Nation). Then some Labor senators joined in. The clapping hands grew in number and volume and senators rose to their feet. I saw Penny Wong gesticulate to her backbenchers and all Labor Senators stood and applauded.

It started out as an unusual, but genuine, acknowledgment of Brandis's classy performance, but it was more than that. As the applause thundered around the chamber for what seemed like minutes, it became, to me, a tangible rejection of racism and hatred designed to deride the Hansonites. They looked sillier by the minute.

When Senate President Parry finally regained order, after letting it run for ages, Senator Wong rose on a point of order.

She said, 'My point of order is this: if I had the opportunity, I would move to congratulate the leader of the government for that statement. And I make this point on behalf of all of us on this side of the chamber: it is one thing to wear religious dress as a sincere act of faith; it is another to wear it as a stunt here in the Senate chamber'.

To my mind, the issue of Pauline Hanson's abuse of the Senate was so serious that I actually wrote to President Parry, on a couple of issues, and said:

Mr President. When the Senate resumes on Monday, September 4, I plan to seek leave to make a short, personal statement concerning my eligibility under Section 44 and any decision to refer that validity to the High Court, acting as the Court of Disputed Returns. I hope leave is granted.

There is another issue I had planned to raise on our first day back concerning Senator Hanson's burqa stunt last session.

Below is what I had planned to seek leave to say. On reflection, although I still believe my points remain valid, it was never my intention to embarrass you or cast aspersions on your hard-working and diligent Clerk.

A better way to handle it, perhaps, would be for you to make some clarifying comment from the Chair.

Right now, there is a discrepancy between what you told the Senate and what Senator Hanson has been telling the media.

With respect
Derryn Hinch

The undelivered Senate speech went thus:

Point of order, Mr President. I'm not sure if this is a point of order or if I should seek permission to make a short personal statement. But it is a procedural matter involving yourself.

Near the end of the last Senate sitting, you made a statement from the chair that you had been assured by the Clerk that the person sitting in Senator Hanson's seat, disguised in a burqa, was in fact Senator Hanson.

Since then, Senator Hanson has pointedly told media that her identity was never checked that day when confronted by the Clerk as she entered the chamber. That she did not speak. That she did not show identification. And, she has claimed, the Clerk merely took the word of her One Nation colleague, Senator Burston, that the person in the costume was, in fact, Senator Hanson.

Mr President, my question is: Did you mislead us or did the Clerk mislead you? Or is Senator Hanson again gilding the lily?

The president *did* address the burqa issue when the Senate resumed sitting but virtually turned it back on the Senate itself to decide what was appropriate or inappropriate apparel. (There were already in place rules on props and paraphernalia.)

Coincidentally, I am on an all-party Senate 'working committee'—instigated by me and the Liberal Democrats' David Leyonhjelm and chaired by President Parry—to try to streamline time-wasting Senate procedures.

As outlined in my diary, we want to bring the upper house more in line with 'the other place'. Get rid of boring, filibustering 20-minute speeches. Trim adjournment speeches to five or ten minutes. Drop the second 'supplementary' question in question time. It doesn't exist in the House of Reps, and makes the Dorothy Dixers from government backbenchers sound cloying and embarrassing.

There is another, admittedly not subtle, agenda. The major parties have to accept that more than a quarter of the men and women in the Senate now represent minor parties or are independents. And, I believe, that percentage will grow at the next federal election.

We demand more speaking time on the floor. Even though, technically, I represent 6 million Victorians, I only get to ask a question of a government minister six or seven times a year during question time. I alternated with Tasmanian senator Jacqui Lambie.

We do get other chances during committee debates on the floor and we can go into the lottery for, what are known as, MPIs—matters of public importance. It is a lottery, drawn by the Senate president every day at 8.30 a.m. But, in recent times, the major parties (and the Greens) have stacked the draw against the 'little guys' by putting nine to twenty 'raffle tickets' into the daily draw.

Recently I won my first, and only, MPI in a year, and launched a good debate on the slaughter of endangered dugongs and sea turtles under the antiquated, and dangerous, protection of native title. Even then, I had to share the two hours with the Lib Dems.

The time we really get to grill ministers, their department heads and others, is those ubiquitous Senate estimates. These hearings, which run for a week or two at a time twice a year (with days starting at 9 a.m. and finishing 11 p.m.) are marathon fiscal grillings that created public reputations of fearlessness for well-prepared senators like Bronwyn Bishop and John Faulkner.

It's meant to be the time we can poke into the government's money cupboard, but 'the reality is'—as Josh Frydenberg says five times in every appearance he makes on Sky News—it is open slather.

An estimates appearance is so feared by some public servants that federal departments have spent hundreds of thousands of taxpayers' dollars on dummy runs. On mock hearings.

At one estimates hearing, after I read that, I asked anybody in the room who had received such training to put their hand up. About twelve people did—including the department secretary sitting at the head table. It raised a huge question in my mind: do public servants have to be coached before appearing in public and merely being asked to tell the truth?

It was an estimates hearing that prompted one of the major headlined brouhahas of my first year as a senator.

My favourite Senate standing committee is the Legal and Constitutional Affairs Committee. I am not a full-time voting member but a 'participating senator' with the right to submit dissenting reports and to have full accreditation, and to be part of that 'open slather' at estimates.

I like it, and attend more meetings than most fully-fledged major party members, because we cover everything from attorney-general Senator George Brandis's memory lapses about the Bond–Bell–WA government tax scandal, to the treatment of refugees on Nauru and Manus Island.

My personal estimates saga involved that committee, and several confrontational appearances by controversial, headline-attracting human rights commissioner Gillian Triggs.

The late, and brilliant, cartoonist Bill Leak from *The Australian*, was accused of being racist, due to a cartoon that depicted an Aboriginal man holding a beer can and unable to remember his son's name. Leak and his newspaper were the subject of complaints to the Human Rights Commission for allegedly breaching section 18C of the *Racial Discrimination Act*.

The cartoonist told the ABC's, now-scrapped, *Lateline*:

I think 18C is an abomination. Look, I can only assume that a lot of people genuinely believe that freedom of speech means the legal right to hurl abuse. In fact, nothing could be further from the truth. Freedom of speech is what created our civil and free society. It is all about the exchange of ideas, about letting people express their views in the marketplace of ideas.

I, too, thought 18C was an 'abomination', and voted against it. We lost. I found including the emotive words 'insult' and 'offend' in legislation insulting. I thought, and still think, current defamation laws, and laws against threatening violence, are sufficient safeguards. And that it's illegal to shout 'Fire!' in a crowded theatre.

I was appalled at the number of supposed free speech champions—journalists and academics—who signed newspaper petitions attacking Bill Leak. A cartoonist, for crissake!

This wasn't long after people had been marching in the streets, in capitals around the world, protesting against the *Charlie Hebdo* massacre in Paris. I went on Sky News and said, '*Je suis* Charlie—but bugger Bill Leak.'

And that prompted my head-to-head with one Professor Gillian Triggs.

Under questioning at estimates, and I was there, the human rights commissioner claimed that Bill Leak's lawyer had failed to respond to commission requests to justify his controversial cartoon, and that if he had provided 'at least a simple statement', a four-month-long investigation would have been 'terminated much earlier'.

Leak's lawyer, Justin Quill, quickly rejected that evidence and produced correspondence detailing several defences *The Australian*'s editorial cartoonist had wanted to establish under section 18D of the Act.

I then lodged a complaint against Trigg's testimony, which triggered her recall of another hearing. There, Commissioner Triggs had demanded an apology from me for accusing her of misleading the Senate and accused me of deceiving the parliament.

My other estimates clash with Triggs came after she was quoted in *The Saturday Paper*, in an interview with talented media veteran Ramona Koval, calling politicians 'seriously ill-informed' and 'uneducated' and people who didn't understand the concept of a democracy and had 'lost any sense of a rule of law'.

But when she appeared before us, Triggs blamed journalists at *The Saturday Paper* for taking her words 'out of context' and publishing 'inaccurate' quotes. She even claimed that sub-editors at the paper had made up quotes attributed to her name. Triggs said one quote, in which she said she could have 'destroyed' the committee by challenging its authority, had been 'put in by a sub-editor'.

I remember challenging her on that claim and pointing out that, as a former metropolitan newspaper editor, I would sack any subeditor who made up a quote.

The prof stuck to her story until the, justifiably indignant, newspaper produced a tape recording of the Koval interview that verified Triggs's trashy quotes.

Triggs then wrote to the Legal and Constitutional Affairs Committee, asking to 'correct the record' because, 'upon further reflection', the article was accurate. 'I answered questions regarding the article in good faith and based on my best recollection.'

It was not her finest moment in a tumultuous and controversial five-year career, which the government was keen to see end.

Speaking of careers ending. One of the most significant, and continuing, events of this parliament is what happened in the dying months of the last parliament. Specifically, the ousting of 'dead man walking' prime minister Tony Abbott by former opposition leader Malcolm Turnbull. Tossed onto the reject heap because he had lost thirty public opinion polls in a row to Bill Shorten. How many is it for you now, Malcolm?

After he was rolled, Abbott (singing from the hypocritical Kevin Rudd hymn book) said: 'My pledge today is to make this change as easy as I can. There will be no wrecking, no undermining, and no sniping. I've never leaked or backgrounded against anyone. And I certainly won't start now.'

Start? He never stopped. To me, the most insidious and invidious example of Abbott's carping and undermining of his own government was in London in October 2017, when he invoked the name and reputation of Cardinal George Pell.

It prompted me to post on the Justice Party Facebook page:

> People in the United States are starting to ask if Donald Trump is losing his marbles. Closer to home I'm starting to wonder if the same question could be asked of our former prime minister, Tony Abbott.
>
> In this week's speech, to the Royal Institute of International Affairs in London, he went back to his old line that climate change is 'crap' and said global warming could actually be doing more good than harm.
>
> He also made a calculated comment about George Pell—the third-most senior cleric in Abbott's Catholic faith.
>
> I have to be careful here because there is a court case going on in Melbourne but in London Abbott gave Cardinal Pell a public character reference by saying:
>
> 'Thank you for giving me the same platform that you've previously given to fellow Australians John Howard and George Pell. I will

strive to be worthy of their example and their friendship …'

Their example? Their friendship? It reminded me of the time a young Abbott gave a character reference for a former fellow seminarian facing sex abuse charges.

Recently, in a message left on my phone about another matter, our former PM advised me to 'shut the fuck up'.

I suggest he take his own advice. DH.

Abbott's comments were in the news again when another former prime minister, Julia Gillard, gave the Annual Hawke Lecture in Adelaide, and started talking about the election of Donald Trump as president, and Brexit and an 'age of anxiety'.

On Paul Murray's eponymous Sky News program, I was asked about former prime ministers airing their views, and mentioned the explicit 'STFU' phone message I'd received. I suggested Tony Abbott, the man we used to dub the 'Mad Monk', should take his own advice. I'll concede that a lot of Twitter trolls thought the Abbott instruction to me was truly sage. Some thought I'd made it up—'fake news', as The Donald would say.

I had played it to five staffers and also in a 'Guess who?' quiz with my former *Hinch* TV producer Dermot O'Brien, at a regular lunch catch-up at Romeo's in Toorak two days after it happened.

I later tweeted to the sceptics: *For disbelievers. Tony Abbott's recorded 'Hinch STFU' comment was on Thursday June 22 after comments on 3AW and PM Live. Hey, ask Tony.*

What Abbott does next is anybody's guess. His obsession with destroying Turnbull—even if it puts his team in the outer paddock and Shorten into the Lodge—is palpable. I believe that *he* believes there is a road back to the party leadership.

Which, I guess, gives me a (not-too-subtle) end to this diary—a segue into 2018. Whither Malcolm? Can the Libs buck the relentless run of negative opinion polls and thwart, what most pundits predict, is an inevitable Labor win in late 2018 or (more likely) early 2019 (when I will also be up for an attempted re-election)?

I often use the term 'Hinch's Hunch'—and I always attach the disclaimer that I am often wrong. But Hinch's Hunch this time is that the proverbial fat lady has not yet sung.

There's been one word the Turnbull government has, to me, genuinely embraced in this term of government. That word is 'pragmatic'. There are four Horsemen of the (Turnbull re-election) Apocalypse: Turnbull, Mathias Cormann, Scott Morrison, Peter Dutton. And Simon Birmingham fits that mould too.

The PM boasts, and he is right, that the Turnbull government, with a grumpy, recalcitrant Senate, got more legislation passed in a year than the Abbott government did. That's pragmatism for you.

I wasn't there, but I am told that, under Abbott (and guru chief-of-staff Peta Credlin) it was 'my way or the highway'. Especially with the Senate crossbenchers. To confirm that, one of Senator Ricky Muir's staffers told me that he saw Prime Minister Abbott poke Muir in the chest with his forefinger.

Doesn't happen these days. It is refreshing to have a legislation-negotiating session with Senator Cormann. Within seconds of sitting down, the finance minister will be more forthcoming than he ever is in his obfuscating verbiage on the laughably misnamed ABC program *Insiders*.

'Pork it, pork it,' he will say briskly, in that guttural accent, while 'parking' (deleting) a piece of legislation that the crossbench finds unpalatable. And then he'll push for a tick on bits of the bill that can/will get voted through. Success for the government.

One of my early learning curves in Canberra was over PPL—paid parental leave.

I had a clutch of nurses, with babies, protesting against planned cuts and a crackdown on alleged 'double dipping', outside my new office in Queens Road, Melbourne. I went down, and a bunch of us had a 'coffee and converse' in a local cafe. I managed to get the government to extend PPL from eighteen weeks to twenty (and maybe twenty-two) and the cut-in point would be pushed out so that no woman currently pregnant, even by a week, would be penalised.

My staff and I spent weeks on the project. Suddenly it was off the agenda. The government had 'porked' it. Parked it. It wasn't even mentioned in 2017.

To cogently wrap this year-long diary up, and get to some final 2018 predictions, I have to go back to the 2016 campaign, when the fledgling Justice Party barely existed—and, only weeks out from the election, I had seen secret polling showing that while most Australians knew who I was, they did not know I was running for the Senate and an abysmally small amount were going to vote for me.

Now I represent 6 million Victorians. I have been accused of being a Liberal stooge (not true). Been accused of taking money from the CFMEU (yeah, right). Been accused of being in the pocket of 'big business' (didn't see any campaign contributions from it). Been accused of supporting paedophilia because I voted for marriage equality (forget how often I went to jail for naming child molesters) and, more often, just dismissed as a dickhead. Well, the DH initials must mean something.

I promised earlier that I'd wrap up with some predictions for 2018—like domestic power bills being the biggest issue for the government right up to the 2019 federal election. But then I remembered the *Ondine* Curse. To explain it, I have to go back to a legendary Sydney news editor named Lou d'Alpuget, father of Blanche, who was a reporter with me on *The Sun* in Sydney in 1963 and later became biographer and wife of Bob Hawke. Lou, nicknamed 'the seagoing ox', was also the paper's yachting writer. When I was editor of the paper, more than a decade later, I fired him but that had nothing to do with the *Ondine* Curse.

Ondine was an upstart American yacht brought here for the 1962 Sydney–Hobart race. Yachting guru Lou wrote that the yacht did not have a hope in hell of finishing well. It was a nautical lemon. The American boat not only won the race, it won in record time. The seagoing ox is still remembered for that prediction more than fifty years later.

It underscores the Hinch adage that 'when you are right, nobody remembers—when you are wrong, nobody forgets'. So, I would say that Malcolm Turnbull will lead the Liberals into the next federal election. But the shadow of *Ondine* looms large.

Flashback: as a precocious young foreign correspondent, I was summonsed back from New York to Fairfax HQ on Broadway in Sydney. On Mahogany Row (as we journos called it) the general manager, one Robert Percy Falkingham, looked across his highly polished desk and told the callow Hinch he was being appointed Fairfax's New York bureau chief. His comment: 'You've been a lucky young man all your life, Mr Hinch.' I was twenty-six going on thirty-five but I chipped him. I said: 'No, Mr Falkingham. You make your own luck.'

That's why I say now that I'm not lucky to be an Australian senator. I am extremely fortunate. I am honoured. I feel more honoured by it than by anything else in my life.

And that's a pretty special place to be in.

Bring on the next year.